CHINESE
PERCEPTION
OF
THE
WORLD

G. W. Choudhury

University Press
of America™

This book is published as a part of the *International Studies Series* of the Center for International Studies, North Carolina Central University, Durham, North Carolina.

Center for International Studies
North Carolina Central University
Durham, North Carolina

To my father,
the late Golam Mawla Choudhury

TABLE OF CONTENTS

FOREWORD

It is with great pleasure that I write this foreword to Dr. Golam W. Choudhury's book **Chinese Perception of the World** which is being published as the first of a series of publications sponsored by our Center for International Studies under the direction of Dr. Choudhury. The second book in the series will be **Sino-American Relations in the Post-Mao Era** based on papers presented at the third annual conference of the Center.

In terms of his experiences in mainland China and in international diplomacy, Dr. Choudhury is exceptionally well qualified to deal with the concerns of his book in an insightful and informed manner. He has visited the mainland twice—first in 1970 as a member of the Pakistan Cabinet and advisor to the President of Pakistan during the time that the latter served as an "intermediary" between Washington and Peking in the context of former President Nixon's new China policy. In this connection, Dr. Choudhury participated in dialogues with Chinese leaders including the late Chairman Mao and the late Premier Chou En-lai. He went again to China in the summer of 1976 for approximately two months during which time he had opportunities for exclusive interviews with party leaders, industrial workers, leaders of Communes, educators, and officials involved in the formulation of Chinese foreign policy.

Both from the title of his book and from the description of the experiences described above, it is clear that the information base from which he works is, in essence, that which reflects a somewhat official view due to the circumstances under which his contacts were made. Nevertheless, such information has rarely been in print in this country and should afford an interesting, analytical, and descriptive overview of contemporary mainland China's thinking about its status and role in world affairs.

Dr. Choudhury's eminence as a scholar guarantees that his data have been subjected to rigorous analysis and refinement. So whatever conclusions he has drawn or implied have been developed in a thoroughly scholarly and thoughtful manner.

Finally, it should be noted that the views expressed in this book are those of the author only and not necessarily shared by The Center for International Studies or the University.

Albert N. Whiting, Chancellor
North Carolina Central University
Durham, North Carolina

PREFACE

This book is the product of my intensive research, both empirical and academic, for the last several years. In 1975, when I completed **India, Pakistan, Bangladesh, and the Major Powers,** I discussed in detail the Chinese foreign policy and political role in South Asia. Subsequently, in **Brezhnev's Asian Collective Security Plan,** I studied the goals of the Chinese and Russian foreign policies. My experiences in Pakistan from 1967-1971, first as the Director-General (Research) in the Pakistan Ministry of Foreign Affairs and then as a member of the Pakistan Cabinet, provided me with unique opportunities to study the "Chinese perception of the world" from first-hand sources. During this period, I also visited China in November 1970.

I left Pakistan in March 1971 but continued my research on Communist affairs at the Royal Institute of International Affairs in London (1971-1972) and at the Research Institute on Communist Affairs at Columbia University (1973-1976). I have maintained my personal contacts with Chinese friends, and since 1971 I have met regularly the senior Chinese diplomats in London, Washington, New York, and Cairo. These contacts, continuing to the present date, have been of great value in my research and publications on Communist affairs. My Chinese friends have treated me very cordially. It is due to their courtesy that I could pay another visit to China in the summer of 1976, accompanied by my wife, Dilara, who helped me greatly in my research. My second visit to China was very pleasant and productive. I had opportunities of exclusive interviews with the top Chinese foreign policy makers, party leaders, industrial workers, educators, and leaders of the commune. While my first visit in 1970 was a unique opportunity of having dialogues with Premier Chou En-lai and an audience with Chairman Mao, the second visit gave me wide opportunities of observing contemporary China.

I sincerely hope that this study will help in the understanding of current Chinese thinking on world affairs, particularly China's attitude toward the United States and the Soviet Union.

I am thankful to Dr. Donald Zagoria for his valuable comments on the manuscript.

I wish to express my sincere appreciation and thanks to Chancellor Albert N. Whiting for his encouragement and help in research and publications of our Center for International Studies and also in my work.

G. W. Choudhury
Center for International Studies
North Carolina Central University
Durham, North Carolina 27707

INTRODUCTION

On October 1, 1949, Chairman Mao Tse-tung stood in the famous Tien An Men Square in Peking to proclaim to the world, "Today the Chinese have stood up." With these words, he formally announced the establishment of the Chinese Peoples' Republic. In the same speech, Mao declared, "Our nation will never again be an insulted nation."

Mao became the first Chinese leader in nearly two centuries to unify his vast country under an effective and efficient central government. China under Mao also began a new course in external affairs putting an end to a century of national humiliation—exploitation through "unequal treaties" imposed by the Western colonial powers and Japan. Though China was not a colony of any European power, its people suffered from the worst type of denigration and exploitation. Even in the 1930s and 1940s, the Chinese were known as an "opium-eating nation"; in cities like Shanghai, women would offer themselves to foreigners just to earn bread; in the big cities, signboards put up by the colonial powers at clubs and restaurants read, "Dogs and Chinese are not allowed."

Mao immediately launched a series of revolutionary socioeconomic changes which transformed a largely illiterate, predominantly agricultural and feudal China, comprising about four million square miles and one-fourth of the world's population, into a modern and unified China. He established a new regime for his people which revitalized a basic Chinese contrast between *luan* (disorder) and *ho-'pling* (peace): The year 1949 ended a century of *luan* from which all Chinese had suffered.[1] All welcomed Mao's regime, therefore, except the "rich peasants," landlords, and reactionary groups who were liquidated. Mao gave the Chinese a new life, new hope, and above all a new confidence in their destiny.

Nationalism, no less than communism, was the driving force in China from 1930 to 1949. As Senator Mike Mansfield points out in his report on China, after his visit there at the beginning of the post-Mao era, "to restore China's pride as a nation was one of Mao's major goals."[2] In the process, Mao built up new recognition and respect for China, with which 110 nations now have diplomatic relations. The twenty years of frozen U. S.-China relations came to an end when President Richard Nixon, accompanied by his wife, journeyed to Peking in February 1972 to be greeted by a smiling Mao. The American ambassador is still in Taiwan, but his presence there is now a mere formality: The real diplomatic activities between the United

1

States and China are carried on through the liaison offices in Washington and Peking.

By any criteria, Mao Tse-tung may be regarded as one of the greatest and most remarkable statesmen of the twentieth century. One may or may not agree with his teaching, but nobody can deny that any contemporary leader has had greater impact on his people than Chairman Mao has had on a quarter of the world's population during the last two and a half decades. No contemporary leader's revolutionary role has influenced world politics to the same extent as Mao's. Cold war based on the polarity of power between two superpowers is no longer possible; multipolar global systems have emerged, thanks to the rise of China from a semicolonial state to the status of emerging superpower. The Chinese, with their usual modesty, never see their country as a superpower, even in the future, yet no basic issue of world politics, particularly any matter of the Asian-Pacific region, can be considered today without taking China into account.

Under Mao, China has become a state which, for the first time in modern history, has been successful in meeting the basic needs of the people—such as food, clothing, housing, and health care. Moreover, China's egalitarian society, in which human dignity has been restored, offers an important lesson to the Third World. What one normally finds in a Third World Asian or African country is a rich and all-powerful elite composed of "twenty-two"* or fewer fortunate families ruling a human mass of "have-nots." One does not see in China the most familiar phenomenon in a Third World country—hungry children roaming the streets or ailing old people begging for medical care or food.

The two largest Asian countries, China and India, began their new political careers in 1949 and 1947, respectively. Even under the British raj, India had a far better economic infrastructure than did China. After India's independence, Nehru's policy of nonalignment made India the most "eligible bachelor in world affairs." During the heyday of the cold war, India received massive external aid both from the United States and the Soviet Union. China's economy, on the other hand, was totally destroyed in 1949 by the Japanese war and then by its own civil war. China could not get massive external aid either; the only source of modest help was the Soviet Union, but

---

*The reference is to the twenty-two families who dominated Pakistan's economic and political life during the 1960s and 1970s. See the author's *The Last Days of United Pakistan*.

2

that aid was arbitrarily and unilaterally withdrawn when China refused to bow down before the "new Czars" at the Kremlin. An impartial comparison, however, of the socioeconomic conditions of these two large Asian countries will show that, in India, there is still widespread hunger, disease, and lack of medical facilities, with the majority of the population living below the subsistence level. In China, one does not hear any longer of death from starvation. The Chinese enjoy a fairly good standard of living compared with that of the rest of the Third World.

In economic development, China has achieved a remarkable record of growth over the past decade. However, one might add that the Chinese under Mao achieved this success at the cost of freedom of speech and other fundamental rights integral to a liberal Western democratic society. The pertinent question is, have the Chinese really made any such sacrifices? China was ruled by feudal emperors and warlords for centuries, then became a victim of colonial exploitation and of occupation by Japan. So the Chinese really did not sacrifice freedoms in return for Mao's "People's Democratic Dictatorship"; they began to enjoy new freedoms—those from hunger, poverty, and exploitation.

Chapter I

China's Quest for Security

A country's foreign policy, or its perception of the world, is not formulated and executed in a vacuum. Every country has to develop its foreign policy in the light of certain basic factors, such as the geopolitical realities of the region in which it is located, its search for security, its needs for economic development, and its ideological background and affinities. An analysis of China's current foreign policy will indicate certain objectives which have governed it since 1949.

The prime objective of China's foreign policy has been national security. The quest for security is a universal phenomenon of all states, even superpowers, but for China this problem has had particular significance and urgency from the time of its confrontation with the most powerful nation of the world, the United States, in an indirect war in 1951. Then from the late 1950s to 1969, China had a strained relationship with both the superpowers, the United States and the Soviet Union.

China has not enjoyed "freedom from fear"—one of the four fundamental freedoms embodied in the famous Atlantic Charter formulated by President Franklin Roosevelt and Prime Minister Winston Churchill in the midst of World War II. Premier Chou En-lai told Pakistan's President Ayub, on March 3, 1966, that "both the United States and the Soviet Union had the common objective of weakening and isolating China." He added that "in a future global conflict, the United States, the Soviet Union, and also Japan and India will be fighting against China; the main target will be China."[3] Chairman Mao also told Ayub, "the United States and the Soviet Union are now trying to have some sort of understanding so as to follow a policy of containment against China."[4] On an earlier visit in 1956, the Pakistan prime minister, Suhrawardy, who was trying to justify Pakistan's adhesion to SEATO by saying that "Americans are not enemies of China but only afraid of China's designs in Asia," was told by Chairman Mao, "If, because the United States is afraid of us, they must control the Philippines, Thailand, and Japan, then we can say that, because we are afraid of the United States, we must control Mexico, Nicaragua, and even Pakistan."[5]

The most populous country of the world (China) and the most powerful country (the United States) were drawn into the Korean War within a couple of years of the end of World War II. Whether Mao was a willing partner in the Korean War or pressured by Stalin to engage in it is a matter of great speculation. The fact that Stalin

7

was not happy to see the unified and powerful China which emerged in 1919 is now almost beyond doubt. Stalin probably would have been happier to see a North China under a Communist regime and a South China under Chiang Kai-shek.[6] It is difficult to assess correctly how sweet or sour were Mao's relations with Stalin. It may be safely presumed, however, that, even before the current Sino-Soviet rift, the Sino-Soviet relaionship was not free from strains and stresses. One of Mao's major policy statements made in April 1956, which was released on December 25, 1976 by Chairman Hua Kua-feng, states, "At the time of the war of liberation, Stalin first would not let us press on with the revolution, maintaining that if civil war flared up, the Chinese nation ran the risk of destroying itself. Then when fighting did erupt he took us half seriously, half skeptically. When we won the war, Stalin suspected that ours was a victory of the Tito type, and in 1949 and 1959 the pressure on us was very great."[7] My own extensive reading of the Sino-Pakistan summit-level dialogues of 1963-1971 has convinced me that Mao was neither willing nor prepared to enter into the Korean War, which proved costly to the Chinese and also initiated twenty years (1950-1970) of hostile and frozen relations between China and the United States.

For a brief period in 1944-1945, Mao sought the friendship of the United States. The Communist party's official newspaper stated in a friendly editorial, "The work which we Communists are carrying on today is the very same work which was carried on earlier by Washington, Jefferson, and Lincoln."[8] John Paton Davis, in **Dragon by the Tail,** referred to the fact that Mao and Chou En-lai "secretly tried to arrange a meeting in Washington with the American president" in January 1945.[9] Donald Zagoria, the reputed scholar of Sino-Soviet affairs, in his testimony on November 19, 1975 to the House Subcommittee of Future Foreign Policy Research and Development, referred to "Chinese efforts at detente with the United States." He noted, "For a summary of the evidence, as late at the spring of 1949, Mao was trying to develop closer ties with the United States in order to avoid falling completely into the Soviet orbit."[10] He also referred to a series of conversations that took place between the American ambassador, J. Leighton Stuart, and Huang Hua during the spring of 1949. Zagoria added, "Mao, for his part, is a 'national Communist' who has always placed the interests of China above those of the Soviet Union and, first in 1944-1946 and again in 1949, sought to balance his relationship with the United States. Mao's efforts to cultivate Washington between 1944-1946 proved unsuccessful once the

United States intervened on behalf of the Nationalists in 1947; similarly, Maoist initiatives as late as the spring of 1949 came to nothing when the United States adopted a policy of nonrecognition of China."[11]

The Sino-American talks were not successful. The U. S. government, while trying for an understanding between the Nationalist and the Communist forces to avoid the civil war, continued to help General Chiang Kai-shek with military aid to the amount of $2 billion. On August 4, 1949, on the eve of the final Communist victory, the U. S. government issued a "White Paper on China" in which Secretary of State Acheson, in a letter of transmittal to the President, blamed the Nationalist debacle on the inept leadership of the Kuomintang rather than on any insufficiency of American aid. Acheson said that, "the only alternative open to the United States was fullscale intervention on behalf of a government which had lost the confidence of its own troops and its own people." He asserted that intervention on the scale required to overcome the Communists would have been "resented by the mass of the Chinese people, would have diametrically reversed our historic policy, and would have been condemned by the American people."[12]

On January 5, 1950, President Truman announced in Washington that the United States would "not provide military aid or advice to Chinese forces on Formosa." Secretary of State Acheson, elaborating for the President, explained that the Nationalists on Formosa were able to obtain all required military equipment by themselves. All they needed, Acheson said, was the "will to resist." The Secretary added that the President's decision was proof to the world that the United States would keep its promises not to meddle in the internal affairs of China.[13]

U. S. sympathy for the Nationalist government headed by Chiang Kai-shek led Mao to draw the distinction between real friends of China and "friends with honey on their lips and murder in their hearts. Who are these people? They are imperialists who profess sympathy with China. However, there are friends who have real sympathy with us and regard us as brothers. Who are they? They are the Soviet people and Stalin."[14]

In spite of Stalin's lukewarm attitude to the Chinese Communists, Mao had no option but to look to Moscow for whatever help and assistance he could procure. He made the following foreign policy statement on April 24, 1945, which appeared later in **On Coalition Government.**

> The Communist party of China agrees with the Atlantic Charter and with the decisions of the international conferences of Moscow, Cairo, Teheran, and the Crimea, because these decisions all contribute to the defeat of the Fascist aggressors and the maintenance of world peace.
>
> The fundamental principle of the foreign policy advocated by the Chinese Communist party is as follows: China shall establish and strengthen diplomatic relations with all countries and settle all questions of common concern, such as coordination of military operations in war, peace conferences, trade, and investment, on the basic conditions that the Japanese aggressors must be completely defeated and world peace maintained, that there must be mutual respect for national independence and equality, and that there must be promotion of mutual interests and friendship between states and between peoples.
>
> The Chinese Communist party fully agrees with the proposals of the Dumbarton Oaks conference and the decisions of the Crimea conference on the establishment of an organization to safeguard international peace and security after the war. It welcomes the United Nations conference on international organization in San Francisco.[15]

Finally, in **On the Peoples' Democratic Dictatorship**, Mao declared that his government would form an alliance with the Soviet Union.

> You are leaning to one side. Exactly. The forty years' experience of Sun Yat-sen and the twenty-eight years' experience of the Communist party have taught us to lean to one side, and we are firmly convinced that in order to win victory and consolidate it we must lean to one side. In the light of the experiences accumulated in these forty years and these twenty-eight years, all Chinese without exception must lean either to the side of imperialism or to the side of socialism. Sitting on the fence will not do, nor is there a third road.[16]

> We oppose the Chiang Kai-shek reactionaries who lean to the side of imperialism, and we also oppose the illusions about a third road. Let readers refer to Dr. Sun Yat-sen's testament: his earnest advice was not to look for help from the imperialist countries but to "unite with those nations of the world which treat us as equals." Dr. Sun had experience; he had suffered, he had been deceived. We should remember his words and not allow ourselves to be deceived again. Internationally, we belong to the side of the anti-imperialist front headed by the Soviet Union, and so we can turn only to this side for genuine and friendly help, not to the side of the imperialist front.[17]

Chairman Mao journeyed to Moscow on December 16, 1949 and was followed by Premier Chou En-lai on January 20, 1950. After prolonged negotiations lasting for two months, a thirty-year Sino-Soviet treaty of "Friendship, Alliance, and Mutual Assistance" was signed on February 14, 1950. It contained two main agreements: (a) that after the signing of a peace treaty with Japan, and in any case no later than the end of 1952, the Soviet Union would transfer Soviet-occupied properties in Manchuria to the Chinese government and would withdraw Soviet troops from Port Arthur; and (b) that the Soviet Union would grant China a $300 million loan for industrial equipment.

U. S. Secretary of State Acheson declared immediately, on February 15, that the treaty would turn China into a "Soviet satellite." The *New York Times* disclosed some alleged "secret clauses" of the treaty which would enable the Soviet Union to turn China into another satellite, resembling the countries of Eastern Europe.[18] Mao, however, disclosed in 1960 that Stalin had held up the signing of the treaty of alliance for two months because he feared that the Chinese Communists, like the Yugoslav Communists, would pursue an independent policy and that he had not begun to trust the Chinese until after the Korean War.[19]

The emergence of a Communist China under Mao in declared alliance with the Soviet Union caused anxiety in Washington, particularly at a time when the East-West cold war tensions were at their height. In Asia, however, notably in India (which China fought in 1962 and which became a close friend of the Soviet Union during the height of the subsequent Sino-Soviet rift in the 1960s and 1970s), the rise of a strong China was greeted enthusiastically. Many Asians looked upon the emergence of a new and powerful China as the great feat of the spirit of Asian nationalism, not as the triumph of international Communism controlled and directed by the Kremlin.[20] Nehru, for one, believed that China and India could form a third force in the world to act as a bridge between Moscow and Washington[21] —an immature assessment, as Mao at that time did not believe in any friendship or alliance with a bourgeois Asian regime like the Nehru government in India.

In the initial years of Chinese nationalism (1949-1952), foreign policy was dominated by doctrinaire and ideological considerations. The focal point of China's foreign policy was its alliance with Moscow. This was the period of the concept of the "world of two camps." It was a period of ideological intransigence and revolutionary militancy for the Communist world. As China was then under the Soviet influence and desperately needed Soviet assistance both for security and for economic development, Mao seemed to follow the Soviet policy of treating the newly independent Asian countries, like India and Indonesia, as "stooges of Anglo-American imperialism." This initial, distorted attitude of China toward the governments of new Asian countries was more in deference, then, to the Kremlin than to China's own thinking or wishes. China, in fact, recognized the realities and dynamics of the new countries in Asia much sooner than did the Soviet Union, whose rigid and indifferent attitude began to change only after Stalin's death in 1953. China's friendship with India during

11

the Korean War is an illustration of China's policy of "uniting with revolutionaries" being transformed into a policy of "union with all." Though China has long been a magnet to its Asian neighbors, it has no desire nor the ability to seek hegemony in Asia. No doubt, it perceives Asia as its natural cultural domain, an area in which it must eventually have a role which is crucial in the search for stability there.

Let us now turn back, however, to the Korean War, which broke out on June 25, 1950. On October 25, 1950, when the UN forces were rapidly moving toward the Chinese frontier, the Chinese troops entered the war, and the intention of the United States "not to meddle in the internal affairs of China," as announced by Dean Acheson, came to an end. The Sino-American relationship was no longer indifferent or unsympathetic but became hostile. The Korean War, which lasted three years and took 150,000 American lives, moved the United States from a position of neutrality or noninvolvement in Communist China's affairs to an active policy of weakening and isolating China. China's problems of security and defense, therefore, became intense.

The exact origin of the Korean War is still obscure and controversial. There is evidence which indicates that the Korean War was basically Stalin's initiative, and Mao was, as pointed out earlier, a reluctant partner. Both Mao and Chou En-lai told Pakistan's President Ayub in March 1965 that the Korean Was was "an unfortunate one," and both made implicit reference to "the Soviet pressures" on China at that time.[22] Chou En-lai also made a distinction between the Korean and Vietnam wars and requested Ayub to convey to U. S. President Johnson that "the situations in 1950 and 1965" were not "similar," that, if the United States would not push the Chinese to a point of no return, "the Chinese would abide by international obligations and responsibilities and would not get involved in any war with the United States."[23] John Paton Davis, a China expert and former U.S. foreign service officer told the House Subcommittee on Future Foreign Policy Research and Development that, if the United States had responded to Mao's gestures toward a Sino-American relationship in 1944-1945 or in 1949, "there would not have been, perhaps, a Korean War, because the whole atmosphere in East Asia would have been quite different, and certainly there would not have been the Vietnam War."[24] However, these are big "ifs."

The Korean War had terrible consequences for China's relations with the United States. It led President Truman to order the defense of Taiwan and subsequently led President Eisenhower to declare, in his first State-of-the-Union message on February 2, 1953, that the U.S. Seventh Fleet would "no longer be employed to shield Communist China."[25] The Seventh Fleet had been present to prevent a possible Chinese attack on Formosa and also any attempt by Chiang Kai-shek to invade mainland Cnina. However, President Eisenhower felt that, after the Chinese intervention in the Korean War, the United States had no obligation to prevent Chiang from attacking mainland China. Hence, Eisenhower's new policy was interpreted in many quarters as "unleashing Chiang Kai-shek," who was still having wild dreams of conquering mainland China.

Eisenhower's statement caused dismay in many Asian countries, such as Japan, India, Pakistan, Indonesia, Burma, and Ceylon. Even the NATO allies, such as England and France, were worried. In the British House of Commons, British Foreign Secretary Anthony Eden described Eisenhower's new policy as having "unfortunate political repercussions without any compensating military advantage."[26] The U.S. Secretary of State John Foster Dulles went further than Eisenhower. China, he said, was an "atheistic Communism" with which no compromise or accommodation was possible.[27] (Emmet John Hughes, in his **Ordeal of Power**, quoted Under Secretary of State Bedell Smith as saying that Dulles was "still dreaming his fancy about reactivating the civil war in China.")[28] The American ambassador in Taiwan was also of the opinion that peace in Asia was impossible until the "predatory regime" in Peking was replaced by a "truly Chinese" government.[29] There were many Americans, however, who were greatly dismayed to see the hostilities grow between the United States and China. Professor John K. Fairbank, for instance, writes, "Only Stalin, perhaps, profited from the Sino-American war in Korea. . . . The Dullesian Cold War against Peking in the 1950s was fundamentally mistaken and unnecessary."[30]

Still, the Eisenhower-Dulles crusade against Communist China continued. China was denied a legitimate seat in the United Nations, which thus was deprived of representation from one-fourth of the world's population. The United States made the UN label China "an aggressor" on February 1, 1951, against the wishes of the Asian countries.

On December 2, 1954, the United States signed a "security pact" with Formosa, which has remained a major complicating factor in the new Sino-American relationship of the 1970s. Following Chou En-lai's threats to Formosa on January 24, 1955, President Eisenhower obtained authorization from the U.S. Congress to use American

13

armed forces to protect Formosa and the Pescadores Islands. The "Formosa Resolution," giving the President the power to use American armed forces against Communist China, was adopted by the U.S. Congress on January 28, 1955; the few dissenting senators, like Wayne Morse, termed it "a predated authorization to wage war." Dulles took it upon himself to form a military alliance against China, and the Southeast Asian Treaty Organization, SEATO, was formed as a result in February 1955. Every Asian country except three—Pakistan, The Philippines, and Thailand—refused to join SEATO; it turned out to be a "paper tiger" with no real teeth. Yet the U.S. policy of containment of China, as demonstrated by the 1954 Formosa Security Pact, the "Formosa Resolution" by the U.S. Congress, and the formation of SEATO, made the Chinese consider the United States an implacable enemy. In his search for security, Mao had to look to Moscow in spite of his grave reservations about the Kremlin leaders, including Stalin.

China began an active diplomacy to win friendship among the newly independent Afro-Asian countries. An especially friendly tie developed between India and China, following Nehru's vigorous support of China during the Korean War; the two countries signed a treaty on five principles of coexistence in 1954. China's next-door neighbors, like Thailand, The Philippines, and Japan, did not respond to China's friendly gestures, but many other Afro-Asian countries were favorably impressed by them at the first Afro-Asian conference at Bandung in 1955.

The huge American military presence in South Korea, South Vietnam, Japan, The Philippines, and Thailand made the Chinese realize how grave were the strategic realities on her frontiers. Before the Korean War, fourteen non-Communist countries recognized Communist China; England, Norway, Denmark, and Finland were the only non-Communist European countries to do so. Thanks to the U.S. policy of containment of China, most of the other non-Communist countries did not recognize China until 1964. In that year, France recognized China, and that event helped China to gain recognition from a number of African countries; by the early 1960s, China had some kind of diplomatic relations with thirty-six African countries. Before China began her new outward-looking diplomatic activities in 1970, after three years of self-imposed seclusion during the Cultural Revolution (1966-1969), it had diplomatic relations with forty-seven countries, including, of course, the Soviet Union and the East European Communist countries (the first to recognize China in 1949).

Thanks to Chou En-lai's successful diplomatic initiatives, China was getting more and more recognition among the countries of the Third World. The greatest setback was the tension between China and India, which began in 1959 and culminated in a war in 1962. But the new relationships with Third World countries did not ease China's search for security. Soon after the Geneva conference on Indo-China in 1954, there were "near-war" situations with the United States in 1955 and 1958 over the off-shore islands of Quemoy and Matsu in the Taiwan strait. By October 1958, however, the crisis in the Taiwan strait was over, and Mao was becoming more cautious about getting militarily involved directly or indirectly with the United States. However, China began to confront new and serious problems in its relations with the Soviet Union. China was finding itself in tense relationships with both superpowers.

Chapter II

The Sino-Soviet Rift

We shall now discuss briefly the Sino-Soviet rift in the context of our analysis of China's foreign policy or perception of the world. The Sino-Soviet rift, one of the great schisms of modern history, is fraught with great strategic and diplomatic implications for the policies of China and the Soviet Union. To begin with, however, it has shattered the monolithic pretensions of international communism. When Mao's Communist China emerged on October 1, 1949, many interpreted it as a monolithic single-willed Communist victory controlled by the Kremlin, but the Sino-Soviet rift has belied many such myths.

The rift has set in motion a chain of far-reaching developments which have affected not only the policies of China and the Soviet Union but also an entire international political system based on polarity of power between two superpowers. It has given rise to the fragile relationship of power between Washington, Moscow, and Peking. It has also had considerable impact on the policies of a large number of Asian and African countries. As Doak Barnet told the House Subcommittee on Future Foreign Policy Research and Development on October 21, 1975, "The split between Peking and Moscow, like the earlier formation of a military alliance between them, must be viewed as one of those historic developments which have seismic effects causing extremely far-reaching changes in broad international configurations of power and patterns of relations."[31]

There is already a mass of literature on the Sino-Soviet rift. Within our short space, we cannot enter into a lengthy discussion of the evolution of the rift, so we shall confine ourselves to the important phases and factors which have bearing on our analysis of China's perception of the world.

From its inception, as we've pointed out already, the Sino-Soviet relationship was not free from tensions. While Hungary, Poland, and Czechoslovakia could be stopped from breaking away from Brezhnev's "commonwealth of socialist countries," China could be neither blackmailed nor blandished. "The ally had become too big to be biddable."[32] Stalin died in 1953. Khruschev, who followed him, had neither the knowledge nor vision of China to keep the uneasy alliance. His abrupt withdrawal of all Soviet technicians and engineers from China in August 1960 was considered by China an act of positive hostility. Earlier, on September 9, 1959, the Soviet Union had taken a *neutral* position in the border disputes between a Communist ally, China, and a non-Communist country, India.[33]

There have been many interpretation of the great schism between the two Communist giants. According to Donald Zagoria, "The

United States has inescapably been a silent, if largely unwilling, participant in the Sino-Soviet dispute."[34] Zbigniew Brzezinski interpreted it in terms of the "two fundamental conceptions of international change: evolutionary change and revolutionary change";[35] according to him, the Soviets favor the former and the Chinese the latter. Robert Scalapino said, "There are three fundamental issues involved in the Sino-Soviet conflict."[36] According to his analysis, the struggle relates to, first, the movement from monolithism to polycentrism within the Communist world: The Soviet Union favors monolithic control while China wants "equality and independence of each Communist party," i.e., "democratic centralism." The second basic issue is the question of "how one treats one's comrades and allies": Distressing to China was the Soviet's neutral stand in the Sino-Indian conflict of 1959 and the delivery of Soviet military supplies to India in 1963-1976, while all aid to "Comrade" China was stopped. Finally, there is the basic issue of "what are the most promising revolutionary tactics and strategies in the twentieth century." The Soviet policy of coexistence with the United States in the early 1960s was considered by the Chinese as "totally incompatible with revolutionary Marxism-Leninism."[37] Another interpreter, William Griffin, referred to "geopolitical factors" and "organizational factors" as the two basic causes of the rift.[38]

Without going into the details of these interpretations by experts and scholars, we may conclude that the Sino-Soviet rift stems from conflicts of ideologies and national interests for two great powers sharing a boundary of several thousand square miles.

In the early 1960s, the rift was no longer secret. First the ideological differences were publicly aired, though not in the polemical way that the current rift is expressed. We have already referred to the Soviet's neutral stand in the Sino-Indian border tensions of 1959 and the Soviet withdrawal of technical aid to China in 1960. The Moscow conference of 26 Communist parties in November 1960 also brought to the public's attention the deep ideological cleavage between the two Communist giants.

When the Sino-Indian border war broke out in October-November 1962, the Soviet attitude to India became a source of great annoyance to Peking. The Soviets, after some initial hesitation, particularly at the time of the 1962 Cuban crisis, began to favor India by giving it huge military supplies, which was interpreted by the Chinese as a hostile action toward themselves. India, the so-called leader of the nonaligned countries, became an important factor in the rift. Indian

Prime Minister Nehru had already declared, "There is no country that cares more about peace than the Soviet Union and no country that cares less than China."[39] The result was the Moscow-Delhi detente, which blossomed into a deeper and warmer relationship between the two countries after the Sino-Indian war. On the other hand, India's "enemy number one," Pakistan, turned to Peking, and this in turn brought forth one of the major political miracles of modern times: the close and special relationship between China and Pakistan, the latter being known as the most "allied ally in Asia" of the United States. This friendship between China and Pakistan shook up the South Asian triangle. Chou En-lai told Ayub in March 1965 that, after the 1959-1960 Sino-Indian differences on the border issue, Chou went to Delhi to negotiate with Nehru, but Nehru "was not in an accommodating mood because he was assured of the Soviet support." "The Soviet Union," Chou added, "encouraged the movement of Indian troops in 1962."[40] The joint U.S.-USSR military supplies to India after the 1962 Sino-Indian war also convinced Mao and the Chinese about a "collusion" between the two superpowers for the policy of containment of China. This belief was repeatedly referred to by the Chinese in their close, friendly dialogues with Pakistan during 1966-1969.[41]

Under an agreement signed on October 15, 1957, the Soviet Union promised to supply the necessary scientific information and technical materials to enable China to manufacture its own nuclear weapons. Then Khruschev cancelled the agreement in June 1959. This agreement and its cancellation were kept secret until 1963 when China disclosed this episode as yet another example of the Soviet betrayal of China.[42] In the meantime, Mao expressed China's bitter resentment over the territories ceded to Russia in the nineteenth century and noted that the Russians were concentrating troops along the Sino-Soviet border: "The forty Soviet divisions on the Chinese border are a constant threat."[43]

During March 2-15, 1969, serious armed clashes took place between Soviet and Chinese frontier guards on the Ussuri River, causing considerable casualties. The accounts of the armed clashes issued by the two sides were conflicting, and both governments exchanged strongly worded notes of protest. The Soviet note demanded an immediate investigation and punishment of those responsible for the incident. It threatened rebuffs of "reckless and provocative actions on the part of the Chinese authorities." Similarly, the Chinese note demanded punishment of the culprits and declared China's right to deliver resolute counterblows if the Soviet government continued to provoke armed conflicts.[44]

The press in both countries began a sharp exchange of polemics. Peking's *People's Daily* described Khruschev, Kosygin, Brezhnev, and company as "a herd of swine" and "new Tsars," while the *Red Star* in Moscow denounced Mao Tse-tung as "a traitor to the sacred cause of Communism. . . tainted with human blood" and compared him to Hitler.[45]

By Western estimates, Soviet troops on the Sino-Soviet border numbered nearly forty divisions, many of which had been recently transferred from Eastern Europe. There were between fifty and sixty Chinese divisions, or about 600,000 men. More alarming was the report that the Kremlin leaders were planning a preemptive attack on the emerging Chinese nuclear capability near China's Sinkiang province. In his dispatches during June and July of 1969, the Pakistani ambassador in Moscow reported that the Kremlin leaders had consulted with their Eastern European allies about the contingency plan for destroying China's nuclear capability, while Pakistan's diplomatic sources in Peking indicated China's grave concern over such a preemptive strike by the Russians. The Sino-Soviet relationship seemed to be moving to the brink of war.[46]

The threat of a full-scale Sino-Soviet conflict subsided in due course, but the cold war between the two Communist giants continued with renewed vigor. The Kremlin's policy to contain China was evident in new Soviet diplomatic initiatives with nations on China's periphery, such as Podgorny's visit to North Korea and Mongolia and Kosygin's visit to India, Pakistan, and Afghanistan in 1969. M.S. Kapist, head of the South Asian Division of the Soviet Foreign Office, visited Burma, Laos, Cambodia, and Japan. The visit of the Mongolian Deputy Foreign Minister to Burma, Cambodia, Nepal, India, and Afghanistan in April 1969 was a part of the Soviet-Mongolian campaign against China.

Two New Soviet Moves for the Containment of China

Soon after the Sino-Soviet border clashes on the Ussuri River in March 1969, the Kremlin leaders initiated two significant moves as a part of their policy to contain China: Kosygin's proposal for regional economic cooperation and Brezhnev's plan for a collective security system in Asia. We will first examine Kosygin's proposal.

In early 1969, Kosygin, while on a visit to Kabal, made a proposal for a regional economic group consisting of Afghanistan, India, Iran, and the Soviet Union. The idea of regional cooperation among these countries was not a new one. The United States, which resumed economic aid to Pakistan and India in 1967 after the 1965 Indo-Pakistan War, had encouraged this idea on the subcontinent, and Pakistan had supported it as soon as it understood that regional cooperation would help its own development, as well as that of Iran and Turkey. But Kosygin's apparently innocuous plan for an economic alliance had political overtones: It was intended to consolidate the Soviet Union's position in relation to China in South Asia.

Kosygin made his second visit to Pakistan within a period of thirteen months, in May 1969. During his long dialogue with Pakistan's new President, Yahya Khan, Kosygin put forward his proposal for a regional economic group and urged Yahya to accept it; he stressed its virtues as a means of development of the region. Kosygin was shrewd in stressing solely its economic aspects. The Pakistani government in the past, Kosygin pointed out, had made "vain efforts" with the help of the capitalist countries to eliminate poverty. While Pakistan welcomed Kosygin's offer of Soviet aid for development and trade, Yahya had been warned "to be cautious of involvement in the Soviet Union's more far-reaching economic proposals with political overtones." Kosygin put pressure on Yahya to accept his proposal for a conference of Pakistan, India, Afghanistan, and the Soviet Union at the deputy ministers' level. It was expected that Iran could also be brought into this arrangement. Yahya, a novice in diplomatic dialogues, agreed to Kosygin's proposal but believed he had made no commitment in favor of joining Kosygin's proposed economic group. However, the Soviet premier later gave the impression that Pakistan had endorsed his economic proposals.[47]

In the meantime, the Pakistani Ministry of Foreign Affairs, as well as the military intelligence, pointed out to Yahya the grave implications of the Soviet Union's forming a political group, under the banner of a highsounding economic plan, right on China's southwest flank. The Chinese ambassador called the Pakistani foreign secretary soon after Kosygin's visit to find out the real attitude of Pakistan and was assured in unmistakable terms that "Pakistan will never be a party of any groupings, political or economic, which are directed against China."[48] The Pakistani press also opposed Pakistan's joining a Soviet-sponsored economic plan. Yahya realized his mistake, and when the Soviet ambassador in Pakistan reminded him of his having agreed to join a conference at the deputy ministers' level, Yahya tried to avoid the issue. The Soviet ambassador expressed his government's disapproval and surprise when a Pakistani Foreign Ministry spokesman said on July 10, 1969 that Pakistan would not join any alliance opposed to China "and the Soviet plan was . . . of little economic advantage." The suspicion that Moscow was forming a political alliance against China was the main factor in Pakistan's refusal to join the plan.

In New Delhi and Kabal, Kosygin received a more favorable response, as was evident from the joint communiqué issued after Mrs. Gandhi's visit to Kabul in June 1969. Under an Indo-Soviet agreement signed in March 1970, India agreed to finance a road from Kandahar in Afghanistan (already linked by a road to the Soviet borders) to the Iranian border, to join another road built by Iran to the Gulf port of Bandar Abbas. These plans would give the Soviet Union an outlet, much needed after the closure of the Suez Canal, for its trade to South and Southeast Asia via Afghanistan and Iran, bypassing Pakistan. In July 1970, the Soviet Union also completed another sector of highway in Afghanistan ultimately capable of linking the Soviet Union with modern roads south to Pakistan.[49]

Brezhnev's Asian Collective Security Plan and China

One of the ironies of the Soviet's feud with China is that it led the Soviets to follow the very policy, espoused by John Foster Dulles, which it had condemned for more than sixteen years—the propagation of military pacts.

The Russians and the Indians had discussed the concept of an "Eastern Locarno Pact" in early 1969. Indian Prime Minister Indira Gandhi and others talked in terms of a security plan for Asia, and in this context they proposed such a pact during President Nixon's visit to New Delhi in August 1969. According to reliable diplomatic sources, the Indians made reference to British Foreign Secretary Anthony Eden's proposal, made after the Geneva Conference in 1954, for an Asian pact along the line of the Locarno Pact of 1925.

The proposal, as made by India in 1969, called for a meeting of Asian countries to undertake a guarantee of the territorial integrity, sovereignty, and independence of each nation—although without any obligation to come to each other's assistance in the case of a violation of the territorial integrity of any member. The major powers were to accept similar obligations which would also not entail any responsibility or commitment for military assistance. India's plan was a sequence to its well-published campaign for a "no war" pact with Pakistan. Pakistan found this proposal unacceptable without a settlement of the Kashmir dispute. India, with the cooperation of their "partners in peace," the Soviets, now tried to expand the idea by applying it to other Asian nations. India also discussed with the Russians the concept of a "Litvinov Protocol" which the Russians had suggested to the League of Nations. When Pakistan pointed out the omission of the Kashmir problem in the 1969 Russian-Indian version of the Locarno Pact, the Russians had no suitable reply, and the idea of such a pact was allowed to die. The Indo-Soviet discussions, with regard to an Eastern Locarno Pact, of a Litvinov Protocol were the precursors of Brezhnev's collective security plan for Asia.[50]

The Soviets had already started to think in terms of a security arrangement for Asia early in 1969 after the fighting on the Ussuri River. Three months after this conflict, on May 29, 1969, the Soviet newspaper *Izvestiya* appeared with an article signed by V. V. Matveyev, entitled "A Filled Vacuum," which gave the first, albeit rather vague, account of a "Collective Security Plan for Asia." Matveyev's 600-word article referred to the British withdrawal from their bases in the Persian Gulf area, the Far East, and the Indian Ocean area which would take place by the end of 1971. He ridiculed the concept of a "vacuum": "A vacuum is an empty space. . .the use of this term in reference to our planet is altogether inappropriate today." He also referred to the "machinations of the imperialistic, expansionist forces" of Americans, Australians, and Japanese as well as of those of the Chinese: "Mao Tse-tung and his associates have definite designs on several countries in the area while supporting the notorious 'vacuum' thesis," he said. He then proceeded to state there would be no vacuum to fill. He concluded that India, Pakistan, Afghanistan, Burma, Cambodia, Singapore, and other Asian countries were making efforts to consolidate their sovereignty and strengthen their economic autonomy. He also stated that Asian nations could best resist interference from foreign powers by setting up the "foundation for collective security in this region."

Matveyev's article was followed by Leonid Brezhnev's lengthy speech at the International Congress of Communist and Workers Parties on June 7, 1969. Brezhnev began his speech with a withering attack on imperialism and Maoism. "We are in unanimous agreement that imperialism as a social system has been and remains the principal obstacle in the historically inevitable movement toward the triumph of freedom, peace, and democracy." He then continued with a similar attack on Maoism. Brezhnev claimed that "the socialist orientation of a number of young African and Asian nations is an important achievement."[51] What is the best guarantee for the young nations of Asia against those "who would like to bind the chains of a new slavery around the young national states?" Brezhnev, who consolidated the theory of "neo-colonialism" in Eastern Europe, after the Soviet military adventures in Czechoslovakia in 1966, with his concept of a "Socialist Commonwealth of Nations," gave the new formula to Asian countries to protect their independence and sovereignty: a system of collective security in Asia. After two decades of constant preaching against military pacts or blocs, Brezhnev now found virtues in this type of military alliance for the Asian countries.

Neither Brezhnev's speech nor Matveyev's article gave any definite idea as to the nature, purpose, and tasks of an "Asian Collective Security Plan." Its basic content or purpose was deliberately kept vague. So far, the Brezhnev plan was nothing more than a trial balloon. For the next few months the Russians contented themselves with such high-sounding phrases as "non-interference in the domestic affairs of other countries," "non-encroachment on borders," and "extensive development of economy." But it soon became apparent to the Soviet Union's southern Asian neighbors, like Pakistan (which had begun a new era of normalization of relations with Moscow in the mid-1960s), that the Soviet Union was assiduously working toward economic and military arrangements which would serve the Soviet policy of containing China and taking the place of the United States in the Asian Pacific region.

After public announcement of the collective security plan for Asia in May and June 1969, the Kremlin leaders began a policy of "carrot and stick" towards South and Southeast Asian countries to induce them to join the Soviet's economic alliance and collective security plan. Indian Foreign Minister Dinesh Singh discussed the plans with Brezhnev and Kosygin during his visit to Moscow in September 1969 and said, "India welcomes the proposal by the Soviet Union to create a system of collective security in Asia. . . ." The Indian foreign minister sought to minimize the military aspect of the plan by adding, "The essence of the Soviet's plan is the development of cooperation among the Asian countries for the purpose of strengthening peace."[52] However, as a result of India's long-standing opposition to any form of military alliance, Singh had to retreat from his position and, on December 18, 1969, issue a modified version of India's reaction, stating that the Indian government did not believe in the concept of big powers acting as guardians of India's security or that of its neighbors.

The Chinese government and press began a vigorous campaign against the new Soviet moves. When the third ministerial meeting of ASEAN (Association of South East Asian Nations) was held in Malaysia on December 16-17, 1969, Soviet propaganda revived the idea of a collective security plan for Asia. On December 14, 1969, Moscow Radio said that a new regional alliance should be formed with the assistance of and participation by the Soviet Union as a "nation with territories both in Europe and Asia." The aim seemed to be to enlist as many of the Asian states as possible, including such allies of the West as Thailand and The Philippines. On December 26, 1969, Moscow Radio appealed to Japan to play an important role in its collective security plan for Asia, even though Japan had already expressed its coolness towards the Soviet's proposal.

On December 15, 1969, Indonesian Foreign Minister Adam Malik said that there was no need for a collective security system in Asia. Indonesia's rejection was as clear as that of Pakistan, albeit for different reasons. Most of the South and Southeast Asian countries, as well as Japan, were unwilling to join the Soviet's policy of containment of China. They preferred a policy of nonalignment in the new cold war between China and Russia, one they had followed in the 1950s during the cold war between the United States and the Soviet Union.

In August 1970, following the successful conclusion of the Moscow-Bonn negotiations on the mutual renunciation of force, the Soviets began to push the theme of a collective security plan for Asia with renewed vigor. During a visit to Pyongyang for the 25th anniversary of North Korea's liberation from Japanese occupation, a Soviet first deputy prime minister, Kirill Mazurov, expressed the hope that the response of the Asian nations would ultimately be favorable. He claimed that the Soviet's ideas on European security were gaining approval and support from European governments, and he said that, in the opinion of the Soviet government, similar ideas would prove to be quite acceptable to the Asian continent as well. Special attention was paid to the attitude of Japan which was causing, and is still causing, concern in Moscow. On September 10, 1970, Moscow Radio, broadcasting in Japanese, cited the recently signed treaty between the Soviet Union and the Federal Republic of Germany as an example of the kind of step that could be taken to improve the international situation elsewhere, claiming that it would provide a firm basis for the signing of similar treaties among the nations in the Far East. Moscow Radio emphasized the importance of Japan in the collective security plan for Asia to the point of suggesting that, without Japanese participation, the plan could hardly hope to get off the ground. On September 23, however, Moscow Radio raised the bogey of Japanese militarism: Referring to Japan's alleged nuclear aspirations, the Soviets tried to arouse in the smaller Asian nations a fear of Japan's military revival so as to stimulate their interest in the security plan.[53]

The Kremlin leaders never missed an opportunity to push their proposal for Asia's security during 1969-1970, although Asian reaction was not enthusiastic. Moscow's disavowals that the plan was directed against any one state or group of states, and its efforts to play down the possible military implications, did not remove the impression among many Asian countries that the plan was primarily aimed at isolating and containing China, and Chinese diplomatic efforts were put into high gear to counter what was termed the "Soviet Version of SEATO." Most of the Asian nations suspected that the Soviet Union was attempting to further its own aspirations in the Indian Ocean through this scheme. The movements of the Soviet fleet in the Indian Ocean and the completion of yet another sector of highway in Afghanistan, capable of linking the Soviet Union with modern roads south to Pakistan (a route which the Russians might hope to use, in preference to the sea route from Vladivostok, for the delivery of food, naval supplies, fuel, etc., to their Indian Ocean fleet) caused concern regarding the Soviet's expansionist designs.

Malaysia's new Prime Minister, Tun Abdul Razak, preferred a policy of nonalignment rather than his predecessor's pro-Western policy. However, Razak also did not endorse the Soviet's plan. Speaking at the 1970 Conference of Non-Aligned Countries in Lusaka, Zambia, he stated that his country would prefer a plan for the neutralization of Southeast Asia guaranteed by the three big powers—the United States, China, and the Soviet Union. In spite of the coolness of the Asian countries to the Soviet plan, the Kremlin leaders continued to press collective security as a "panacea for all of Asia's current ailments."[54]

Following a Moscow conference of Soviet envoys, the Soviet ambassador to Pakistan called on President Yahya and on the Pakistani foreign secretary in an attempt to sell the Brezhnev scheme.

He described the proposed plan in lofty terms, stressing such features as "non-interference in internal affairs of signatory countries" and "economic, cultural, and scientific cooperation." The ambassador pointed out to the foreign secretary that the inadequacy of economic collaboration under SEATO and CENTO was in contrast to the more worthwhile collaboration possible under the Soviet plan.[55]

However, upon being questioned about the security aspects of the plan, the Soviet ambassador was forced to reveal its main purpose, which concerned not so much economic cooperation as the containment of China. The specifics of the proposed security agreement also made plain the following: The signatories should not enter into any alliance, formal or informal, with a third country that might be hostile to any member nations, nor should they make any commitment inconsistent with the proposed security plan for Asia. The signatory nations "would consult each other in the event of an aggression by a third party." The anti-Chinese slant was also indicated by the fact that Brezhnev announced the plan only three months after the most serious armed conflict to date on the Sino-Soviet borders. Yahya wanted to know what help, if any, the Brezhnev Plan would offer "in case of an aggression committed by one member country against another," such as would be the case in a repetition of the 1965 Indo-Pakistani war. The answer was that "The Asian Security Plan will put an end to such regional conflicts as those encouraged by the imperialist countries like the U.S.A., and by expansionist nations like China."[56]

President Yahya Khan scheduled a five-day visit to Moscow beginning June 22, 1969, and both the Soviet ambassador to Pakistan and Pakistan's ambassador to Moscow indicated that the Kremlin leaders would give top priority to Asia's security system in the discussion. During Yahya's lengthy talks with Kremlin leaders, Pakistan was assured of larger Soviet economic aid for its fourth five-year plan (1970-1975). For example, Soviet assistance was promised for several industrial projects, including a one-million-ton steel smelting plant in Karachi. But when Yahya raised the question of continued arms shipments to Pakistan, the Kremlin leaders demurred. Kosygin told Yahya that he could not expect Soviet arms as long as Pakistan was unwilling to endorse the Asian security system. He added that the system would be the best guarantee for its (Pakistan's) territorial integrity, pointing ominously to an "explosive situation in east Pakistan," "foreign involvement there," and "China's role." Yahya and his advisors in the government disagreed, and Yahya ended the dialogue with a polite but firm rejection of the Brezhnev and Kosygin proposals.[57]

China has always been convinced that it was the target of the Soviet-inspired Asian security system. When Brezhnev announced the plan in June 1969, China denounced it in unqualified terms and expressed concern to its South Asian friend, Pakistan. But the Chinese approach did not resemble the blunt statement of Soviet Defense Minister Marshal Andrei A. Grechko, who threatened Pakistan for "flirting with Mao." The Chinese leaders politely warned the Pakistanis, "We know the Russians better, just as you know the Indians better." Nor did the Chinese try to get any information from Pakistan President Yahya, to whom the Russians gave an adequate account of their proposed security plan in June 1970. The Pakistanis gave unqualified assurances to China that Pakistan would never join any Russian-sponsored security plan which was directly or indirectly aimed against Peking.[58]

President Yahya, as a friendly gesture to China, told the Chinese ambassador, Chang Tung, the substance of his talks with the Russians during his state visit to the Soviet Union in June 1970. The Chinese had other sources of information, but Yahya was perhaps one of the earliest.

The fear of Asian countries that the Soviet Union would involve them in the Sino-Soviet conflict has doubtless been heightened by the way the proposal itself has become a subject of recrimination between Moscow and Peking. The implication that moves toward an arms settlement in Europe might enable the Soviet Union to play a larger role in Asia cannot be reassuring to the Chinese or, hence, to the other Asian countries. The Moscow Radio commentator complained that "Peking's attempts to hamper the relaxation of tension in Europe"—which included its welcoming the enlarged Common Market—could "only do serious damage to the security of Asian nations as well." Chinese opposition to the proposal for an Asian collective security system was criticized on October 11, 1972 in a major article in *Izvestia* by V. Kudryavtsev, author of several other articles on the scheme. Referring to the "correctness" of the principle of respect for sovereignty and the inviolability of frontiers, which is clearly intended to rule out Chinese and Japanese territorial claims, Kudryavtsev said that opposition by the Chinese leaders and Japanese politicians demonstrated the truth of the saying that "an uneasy conscience betrays itself."[59] Chinese counterattacks frequently refer to the alleged military threat from the Soviet Union and create the impression that Moscow has great power ambitions in Asia.

Chapter III

China's New Outward-Looking Foreign Policy
1970-1976

China began its new outward-looking foreign policy after the self-imposed isolation of the great Cultural Revolution (1966-1969). It emerged from seclusion with greatly strengthened party and government machinery, as reflected in 1970 by an ambitious foreign economic aid program designed to secure for China a major stake in world affairs. In the post-Cultural Revolution period (1971-1976), China's foreign policy objectives evidently included (a) improving relations with the United States, as a counterbalance to the Soviet Union; (b) securing a legitimate place in the United Nations and expelling Taiwan from it; (c) winning the friendship of nonaligned countries; and (d) normalizing relations with its East, Southeast, and South Asian neighbors, particularly Japan. China also sought to encourage tendencies toward regionalism in the Balkans, to establish friendly relations with West European and the Middle Eastern countries, and to extend its influence in Africa by intensifying activities where it had already established a foothold.

The ideological motivation of China's more active foreign policy was outlined in a widely publicized article which appeared on November 9, 1971 in the party's theoretical journal, *Red Flag*. The article was part of a press and radio campaign to explain the new cordiality toward the United States and to justify President Nixon's planned visit. Presented as an analysis of Mao's 1940 *On Policy*, it set out the advantages of "a flexible foreign policy" capable of exploiting international tensions and rivalries to advance revolution and explained the need for "various forms of struggle" against the counterrevolutionary policy of the enemy. Mao's 1940 precepts on forming tactical alliances with secondary enemies to defeat the primary one were said to be applicable in 1970-1971—a clear indication that the Soviet Union had been elevated to the first rank of China's enemies. The article also revealed the doctrinal basis of the attempt to assume the leadership of the Third World by cultivating closer friendships in Africa, the Middle East, and Latin America. *Red Flag* cited the "contradiction" between the industrialized and developing worlds as one that China was capable of exploiting in the interests of world revolution.

Sino-American Relations

After two decades of hostile and frozen relations between the United States and China, President Nixon made a big decision in

1969 to normalize these relations. As we have described earlier, the Sino-Soviet relationship, by that time, had moved to the brink of war, so that Nixon's China initiatives could not have been made at a more appropriate time. The President seemed to have concluded that the best chance for the United States to reach an understanding with the Soviet Union lay in keeping open U.S. diplomatic options toward Peking.

Pakistan President Yahya's Grand Assignment

During his 22-hour visit in Pakistan, President Nixon asked Pakistan President Yahya Khan to act as a "courier" between Peking and Washington to find out from Chinese leaders their reactions to Nixon's new initiatives to normalize relations with China. Pakistan was greatly delighted to have this opportunity. The Sino-Pakistan relationship was not only approved by the United States, but the U.S. president sought to utilize it for improving American ties with Peking. It was almost a godsend for Pakistan. I cannot say why Nixon chose the Pakistani president. Nixon knew Ayub and had seemed to have friendly relations with him, but Yahya was altogether unknown to Nixon and was also a novice in diplomacy. Pakistan, of course played a significant role in establishing diplomatic relations between China and a number of countries, including Canada, Iran, and Turkey. U.S. Secretary of State William Rogers had already gleefully reported to Yahya in May 1969 that "China now considers the USSR and not the U.S. as enemy number one."[60] On the eve of Nixon's visit to China, I prepared for Yahya a lengthy note on the growing Sino-Soviet rift, its possible developments, and the possibilities for Sino-American relations in the context of the Yahya-Rogers talks. Nixon knew that, of all noncommunist countries, Pakistan had the most cordial and intimate relations with Peking, and, at the same time, Pakistan still cherished and valued her friendship with the United States. So Nixon's choice was not unwise or inappropriate.

Yahya had an informal discussion about the Sino-American relationship with his top advisers but did not divulge his grand assignment, because Nixon had urged Yahya to do this assignment with "utmost secrecy." The normal diplomatic channel was to be avoided; neither the State Department nor the Pakistan Foreign Ministry would be taken into confidence. Nixon's style of "top-secret diplomacy" was applied here. I do not know how many people in Washington knew about the assignment or, particularly, the substance of the Chinese messages channeled through the Pakistani president to the White House.

In September, Yahya began his job most secretly and also successfully. There were initial doubts about China's reaction. Just a few days after Nixon's visit to Pakistan, a top Pakistani Foreign Ministry official, who became foreign secretary in January 1970, Mr. Sultan Khan, predicted that the Chinese would not react favorably. Sultan Khan, Pakistan's ambassador in Peking till late 1968, told me that China maintained the view that, just as the Indians did not really want to improve relations with Pakistan but were interested in talks only to demonstrate their "peaceful intentions," so the Americans, the Chinese felt, wanted to talk on peripheral issues in cultural relations, trade, etc., but not on substantial issues like Taiwan, a Chinese seat at the UN, or diplomatic recognition.

But the whole situation changed after the Sino-Soviet border clashes of 1969. The Chinese, as I gathered from my careful reading of the Pakistani-China diplomatic dialogues, were very concerned over a "preemptive attack" from the Soviet Union—hence the urge to normalize relations with the United States. Nixon could see the great diplomatic options for U.S. policy as a result of the growing Sino-Soviet rift.

So the messages began to carry cheerful words for Nixon, and Yahya was, of course, greatly delighted by the happy developments which enabled Pakistan to consolidate her ties simultaneously with Peking and Washington.

The Channel

The Chinese ambassador in Pakistan, Mr. Chang Tung, used to carry the messages directly to Yahya and not through the Foreign Ministry. Chang Tung had free and unlimited access to the President's house. Yahya used to write in his own handwriting the substance of messages, keep them in his own custody, then send them through his ambassador in Washington, Mr. Aga Hilali, in double-sealed envelopes (not to be opened by Hilali) to National Security Adviser Henry Kissinger and to Nixon.

The process of negotiations was complicated by the escalation of the fighting in Cambodia in the summer of 1970 and when Prince Sihanouk took shelter in Peking. In some of the messages from Peking during this period, there was again revival of Chinese doubts about U.S. "sincerity." Yahya was upset, and did his best to mollify Chinese doubts. The mutual need and desire for improvement of Sino-American ties, in Washington and in Peking, made it possible for the negotiations to survive such temporary setbacks.

When Yahya traveled to Washington in October 1970 and to Peking in November of that same year, the prospects were brighter. In Washington, Nixon told Yahya that "nobody has occupied the White House who is friendlier to Pakistan than me." In Peking, Yahya had a grand reception (I was a member of his entourage). Yahya had a meeting with Chairman Mao, but the real dialogues on the growing Sino-American ties were held with Chou En-lai in the Peking Guest House, where Yahya was staying. The two conversed exclusively for, at least, fifteen to eighteen hours during Yahya's five-day stay in Peking. Neither in Washington nor in Peking was Yahya assisted by his ambassadors while talking to Nixon and Chou. Kissinger was present during the Washington meeting.

Yahya's services were greatly appreciated both in Washington and Peking. They finally culminated in Kissinger's secret trip to Peking, via Rawalpindi, in July 1971, in the midst of the civil war in Bangladesh. I do not know if the Pakistani President's services were utilized after Kissinger's visit.

After Dr. Kissinger's first secret trip to Peking, Nixon dramatically announced in August 1971 that he would be visiting China for talks with the Chinese leaders. An "eight-point plan" was presented by Chou En-lai to Washington before Nixon arrived in Peking in February 1972. Nixon's visit did not result in an "instant detente"; neither side expected such a miracle. But the Sino-American talks did cover a wide range of issues of mutual concern, such as Taiwan, Indochina, and the alleged revival of Japanese militarism.

The Fragile Triangular Relationship

In the wake of the 1972 Shanghai communiqué, a fragile triangular relationship has developed among the United States, the Soviet Union, and China. While the talks have never been triangular—there have been either U.S.-USSR or U.S.-China talks—the absent third party has always been of crucial importance in Washington's negotiations with both Communist giants. As Winston Lord of the Policy Planning Staff in the Department of State remarked, during

House hearings on future foreign policy research and development, "Our relations with the world's largest country and the world's most populous country are cardinal elements in our pursuit of a more secure and moderate international system."[61] After his visit to China in December 1975, President Ford said, "Our relationship with China is becoming a permanent feature of the international political landscape. It benefits not only our two peoples but all peoples of the region and the entire world."[62] Secretary of State Kissinger, in his speech to the UN General Assembly of 1975, said "There is no relationship to which the United States assigns greater significance than its new ties with the People's Republic of China."[63]

Twice, an American president has paid a visit to China. The secretary of state has held high-level talks with Chinese leaders in both Peking and New York. Members of Congress, scholars, and people from various other spheres of life have visited China. The Chinese have also come to the United States, but no Chinese head of state has yet paid a return visit. The Chinese made it clear that their leaders would not visit the United States as long as the ambassador of the Republic of China has his office in Washington. Both sides freely concede the advantages and benefits of the new Sino-American relationship. From the U.S. side, new ties with Peking mean "improved prospects for preserving global equilibrium, (and) reduced dangers of conflict in Asia, an area where the interests of all the world's major powers intersect."[64] Chinese leaders and their senior diplomats in Washington and at the United Nations acknowledge that the new relationship has reduced the Soviet threat to China and other smaller Afro-Asian countries, temporarily halting Soviet expansionist designs.

When President Nixon seized upon his "China Option" in 1971-1972 and then moved to Moscow through the Asian backdoor, a new global balance of power emerged, one favorable to Washington. Both Moscow and Peking sought U.S. friendship, not out of love for the Americans but out of their growing mutual distrust and fear. If Nixon or Kissinger would go to Peking, Kremlin leaders would be shaky over a "collusion" between the United States and the People's Republic; similarly, the Chinese would worry about the meaning of detente on the occasion of a Nixon-Kissinger visit to Moscow. Leonid Brezhnev was reported to have advised the United States, Britain, and France that the Soviet Union was in no sense worried about present Chinese hostility but added onimously that, by the century's end, "China would be formidable." He proposed a more cooperative

Soviet-Western relationship to block the danger that "Peking, backed by the Third World, might threaten both Russia and the West in another generation."[65]

Brezhnev reportedly warned the West that, if it failed to reach meaningful agreements with the Soviet Union soon, Moscow would have only one obvious alternative: after Mao, restoring the old alliance with China.

For their part, the Chinese leaders made pleas with the United States to unite against "Soviet Social Imperialism," which, according to the Chinese, constitutes the "most dangerous source of war." The Chinese perception of "Soviet Social Imperialism" was summed up as follows:

> Engaged in unbridled aggression and expansion abroad in contending for world hegemony, the Soviet Union inevitably will go to war. Above all, this is determined by its social system. Once a socialist state, the Soviet Union has degenerated into a social-imperialist state ever since the renegade Khrushchev-Brezhnev clique usurped Party and state power and began pursuing a revisionist line, restored capitalism. Having placed itself in the ranks of the imperialist states, the Soviet Union inevitably comes under the basic law of imperialism and is enmeshed in a multitude of inherent imperialist contradictions. Social-imperialism is, therefore, entirely the same as the capitalist-imperialist system, made however, even more rapacious and more truculent in its aggression and expansion abroad.[66]

The early Nixon-Kissinger hope for a "triangular relation" among Washington, Moscow, and Peking has proved immature. Soviet designs in the Middle East, Angola, and the Indian Ocean-Persian Gulf area, coupled with Moscow's huge military build-up, has dashed the early hopes of detente. The rapid expansion of the Soviet armed forces in recent years has alarmed many Western political and military leaders. In February 1976, General Alexander Haig, the Supreme Allied Commander in Europe, expressed his concern in unusually blunt terms. In a briefing for newsmen at Washington's Center for Strategic and International Studies, Haig declared that "the expansion of Soviet military capabilities far exceeds the requirements of a purely defensive posture. The enemy is moving." Haig noted that the Russians have increased their forces on the West European front by 100,000 men in recent years; he also said that the Soviet navy has been transformed into "a global force," while its air force has become "offensive in character." The big build-up, Haig argued, was part of the Kremlin's strategy of "worldwide imperialism," and he warned, "we are getting to the fine edge of disaster."[67] Dr. Henry Kissinger, in his speech at the 1976 session of the UN General Assembly, attacked the Soviet Union on a broad range of issues. He said, "We have been concerned by the continuing accumulation of the Soviet armaments and by the recent instances of military intervention to tip the scales in local conflicts."[68] But both President Ford and Kissinger have told the Americans and the world that the policy of detente with the Soviet Union will be continued. The new Democratic president, Jimmy Carter, and his foreign policy advisors have not challenged the rationale for the policy of detente with Moscow, although they have expressed concern that the Ford-Kissinger policy is "too soft" towards Moscow. It may be assumed the new administration will pursue detente and not revert to the cold war policy of the 1950s and early 1960s.

How the Chinese Assess the Sino-American Relationship

The Chinese, like the American policy makers, attach great importance to their relationship with the United States. The favorable responses Peking made to Nixon's gestures in 1969 came only after thorough and careful analysis of China's national interest and the global balance of power. They were not merely the "brain-product" of one individual, such as the late Premier Chou En-lai, but were made under the guidance of Chairman Mao, who took the leading members of the Chinese Communist party and the generals of the People's Liberation Army into full confidence before making this big decision. It is wrong to assume that Chinese leaders take any major course of action without an adequate assessment of the internal and external factors involved. They may not have an American or British style of democracy, where issues like that are debated in a congress or parliament, but one must not forget Aristotle's saying that there is no universal form of constitution or of government. The Chinese have their own form of proletarian dictatorship. It is futile to expect the decision-making process in a communist state to be the same as in a Western democratic country. Thus, I doubt that the deaths of Chou and Mao will change China's policy toward the United States. Such a turn of events could happen, but I am confident that China's basic foreign policy tenets will not change with these two leaders' disappearance. If the prospect alters, it will be the result of external factors, not because of the so-called power struggle in Peking. China's present policy toward the United States enjoys the approval of the major groups in its leadership.[69]

The Chinese consider the present phase of the Sino-American relationship with anguish rather than with anger. They refer to the United States' informal but clear promises and assurances regarding the Taiwan issue and the consequent establishment of full diplomatic relations. As one who had access to these promises and pledges of 1969-1971, I am inclined to sympathize with China's sense of frustration. Under the 1972 joint communiqué issued at the close of Nixon's visit, the United States acknowledged "that all Chinese on either side of the Taiwan Strait maintain that there is but one China and that Taiwan is part of China." What has this meant? The Chinese made it clear from the beginning that under no circumstances would they accept the concept of "two Chinas": "One China" is an article of faith with them. They have not established diplomatic ties with any country unless that country's ambassador was removed from Taiwan. When the United States began to talk of normalizing relations in 1969-1971, the Chinese made their views on the Taiwan issue known to Washington in unambiguous terms. They also told me that when they agreed to establish a liaison office in 1973, they did so on the understanding that it would soon be upgraded to full diplomatic status. The procrastination of the United States in establishing full diplomatic relations between the two countries has been a disillusionment to China.

The Chinese were happy with the good beginning to Sino-American relations made when Nixon visited in February 1972. From 1972 through 1973, the process of normalization, according to their interpretation, moved satisfactorily. Then came Watergate and the subsequent decline of Nixon's prestige and power. With Nixon's exit, a stalemate seemed to develop in the Sino-American relationship. The Chinese feel now that Nixon could see clearly the dangers from the Soviet Union, and he was therefore anxious to promote better relations with Peking as a counterbalance to the global distribution of power, but with his departure from office, U.S. foreign policy initiatives seemed to move from the U.S. president to the U.S. secretary of state—an assessment to which many Americans would agree. Chinese officials feel that when Kissinger became not only executor but initiator of America's foreign policy, he went back on his past assurances to the Chinese. They were quick to add, however, that what Washington might do or not do in its relation with Moscow "is not their concern." At the same time, they gave clear and unqualified warnings that the United States would be sadly mistaken if the next U.S. administration took Chinese friendship "for granted" or, worse, if the Chinese found that the Americans were using their new China links as bargaining leverages with the Kremlin.

This is a matter of great significance to Americans. The rationale for detente with the Soviet Union has been widely questioned: Zbigniew Brzezinski, Vladimir Petrov, Eugene Rostow, George Ball, Senator Henry Jackson, and Barry Goldwater, among others, have expressed grave concerns about Kissinger's "one-way traffic" to Moscow. Despite detente, the Soviet Union is increasing its military forces faster than is the United States. As former Secretary of Defense James Schlesinger stated, "the future is clouded with uncertainty, but there can be no doubt about the larger and growing capabilities at the disposal of the USSR."[70]

Brzezinski, about whom the Chinese asked me many questions, has said, "It is important for the United States to move toward normalization of relations with the People's Republic of China." He feels that the rapprochement between Washington and Peking launched by Nixon in 1971-1972, "has been somewhat impaired by the Chinese belief that the United States' weakness constitutes appeasement of the Soviet Union designed to deflect Soviet hostility from the west on to China."[71] Brzezinski, who is favorably regarded by the Chinese, seems to have assessed Chinese thinking in a much better way than did Kissinger, who appeared to be in no hurry to upgrade the existing Sino-American relationship. According to the Chinese, Kissinger seemed to have taken China's friendship "for granted." Brzezinski favors taking steps to avoid a cooling of American-Chinese relations, since "such a cooling would free the Soviet Union to pursue tougher policies in Europe, the Middle East, and Africa."[72]

China may not be an ally of the United States, but a strong China, unfriendly to Moscow, is as vital to U.S. global interests as is a stronger NATO, a stronger ANZUS, and a stronger Japan. One should also remember that China is not opposed to a stronger NATO, ANZUS, or Japan. In fact, there are many common objectives, if not an identity of interests, between Washington and Peking—much more so than there are between Moscow and Washington.

The Chinese subtly expressed their disapproval of Kissinger's handling of U.S. foreign policy since 1974. They felt that, as Marxists and former allies of the Russians, they knew the "socialist imperialists" in Moscow better than did the former Harvard professor. They told the Pakistanis in 1964-1965, when Pakistan made serious bids to woo the Soviets, "We know the Russians in a better way, just as you know the Indians better. You warned us against the Indians, and we made a mistake by not listening to you properly."[73] Pakistanis remembered the Chinese warning in 1971, rather too late, when India, backed by the Soviets, dismembered Pakistan. It cannot be denied that the Chinese have a closer historical experience of Soviet aims and methods than Kissinger had, and that their warnings about the Russians deserve serious attention.[74]

The Chinese preferred not to make direct comments on U.S. internal politics in the election year, but they left me with no doubt that they were unhappy with Kissinger's never-ending search for detente with Moscow, which they considered bound to be a failure, even as Neville Chamberlain's policy of appeasement toward Hitler proved disastrous. They seem to favor Brzezinski's views on the Soviet Union and its expansionist designs. The importance of U.S.-Chinese ties has recently been emphasized by Admiral Thomas Moorer, former Chairman of the U.S. Chiefs of Staff, who is certainly not among those Americans who treat China as an "ally." He observes, "The P.R.C. is not on par with the United States or the Soviet Union in the overall power equation...yet China in effect balances Soviet power in Eurasia—at least to the extent of blocking Soviet expansionist ambitions eastward."[75]

American policy makers need to pause at this point and consider the consequences of a possible thaw in Sino-Soviet relations—perhaps as a result of the United States taking China's friendship for granted. The Chinese do not concede that their attitude toward Moscow would be changed by a third party's policy of detente with the Soviet Union. But when I questioned them about their reaction if there should be a real change of the global balance of power as a result of a U.S.-USSR detente, their reply was not ambiguous. Like any other big power, China is constantly reappraising and rethinking world affairs; in this process, Peking's attitude toward Moscow figures prominently. Who can say whether the two Marxist states may come to some closer understanding? There is no inherent risk of a "pro-Moscow" group emerging as a result of Mao's death; that risk exists only if U.S. policy pushes China into a highly unfavorable global balance of power.

In spite of all the talk about detente, the Soviet Union has not missed a single opportunity to undermine U.S. interests in the Third World—in South and Southeast Asia, the Indian Ocean and Persian Gulf areas, the Middle East, Africa, and even in Latin America. Moscow discerns a steady erosion of the position and role of the United

States in the Third World as a result of such factors as the emergence of a Communist Cuba; the deterioration of the United States' influence and political-economic control over its "strategic rear," i.e., Latin America; the collapse of the U.S. venture in Vietnam; the retrenchment of the U.S. global containment policy as reflected in the Nixon Doctrine; the loss by the United States of its assured majority in the United Nations; the growing number of developing countries which have established close relations with the Soviet Union; and the pressure for a new world economic order.[76]

One perspective of the Chinese attitude toward the U.S. role in world affairs was summed up by Elliot Richardson:

> China's leaders want the United States to play a major role in Asia indefinitely, to head off Soviet domination of the region. I don't think the Chinese would want to see any shifts in Asia for the foreseeable future. The Chinese have an interest in the preservation of a major U.S. role toward the rest of the world, if only because Chinese security, to a degree, depends on a continuing American countervailing role against the Soviet Union.[77]

China and the Soviet Union, 1970-1976

During my second visit to China in July-August 1976, I repeatedly asked my Chinese friends if there is any chance of a rapprochement between China and the Soviet Union. The answer in clear and unmistakable terms was always negative. The Sino-Soviet rift, the Chinese told me, has reached a stage at which it cannot be reconciled by a change of leadership in either country. The rift, which began as an idea, is now one of the most portentious international political developments of contemporary world affairs. The Russians have massed a large number of troops on China's borders. The cardinal feature of Soviet policy since the 1969 Sino-Soviet border clashes has been to weaken and isolate China. With some justification, China interprets such Soviet diplomatic moves as the Brezhnev Asian collective security plan and Kosygin's plan for a regional economic group, consisting of Afghanistan, India, Iran, Pakistan, and the Soviet Union, as devices to encircle China with hostile and unfriendly neighbors. The Indo-Soviet entente, closer Hanoi-Moscow links, and Moscow's strong opposition to a treaty of friendship between China and Japan are also interpreted by the Chinese as strategic Soviet actions against them. The growing Soviet naval presence in the Indian Ocean and the Persian Gulf, along with its expansionist designs in Africa, the Middle East, and even in Latin America are matters of grave concern to Peking, as well as to Washington.

43

The Soviets, on the other hand, see China's growing national self-confidence and its broadening impact on world politics as a direct threat to its own national, regional, and world interests. Moscow's strong reaction of propaganda reveals its anger at alleged Chinese distortion of the nature of the struggle between socialism and capitalism, and also the Soviet's anxiety about Peking's attempt to take over the leadership of the Third World and, thus, create a block pitted primarily against the Soviet Union. Chinese maneuverings with nonaligned countries, support for Rumanian sovereignty, and encouragement of Balkan regionalism have aroused particular concern in Moscow. Thus, the Soviet Union has been showing signs of anxiety over what it views as an "insidious campaign" by China to outflank Soviet interests in both Europe and Asia.

After the end of the Vietnam War in 1975, the Soviet Union and China stepped up their propaganda compaigns against each other. Chinese commentators' denunciations hit upon "Soviet expansion in Southeast Asia," a new focus in the growing Sino-Soviet rift. The Chinese press accused Russia of trying to "swallow Southeast Asia at a gulp" and compared Brezhnev to Hitler. "The Soviet-social imperialists have honey on their lips and murder in their hearts," said *Jemmin Jih Pao* in a warning to the people of Southeast Asia.[78] Finally, the Chinese commented in the following way on the Soviets' role in Angola:

> On the pretext of opposing imperialism and colonialism and supporting the national-liberation movements and revolutionary struggles, they stretch their tentacles into other countries to carry out colonialist domination and exploitation. By forming military blocs, concluding friendship and co-operation treaties, and making great use of economic and military aid, they try hard to control and enslave not only the Third World but also the Second World countries. And when they fail to achieve their ends by peaceful means, they resort to military coup d'etat, subversion, and even direct armed intervention and aggression in these countries.[79]

The Soviet Union, for its part, expressed displeasure at Chinese efforts to develop closer ties with both Western Europe and Japan. Specifically, the Soviet Union was upset by China's plan to open up relations with the European Common Market and by Peking's support for a stronger military and economic alliance in Western Europe, interpreting it as a deliberate subversion of Soviet efforts to promote understanding between Eastern and Western Europe. The late Soviet Defense Minister Andrei A. Grechko told a military conference in May 1975 that "Western imperialists were establishing a united anti-Soviet front with the participation of China."[80]

The Strategic Factor

The most dangerous aspect of the Sino-Soviet rift is the presence of forty-five to fifty-five divisions of armed forces on each side of the Sino-Soviet border. A great deal of the Soviet build-up has been devoted to the construction of barracks, roads, rail links, and permanent training grounds near the border. The Soviet forces include surface-to-surface missiles and 500-mile-range scaleboards.[81] According to a 1973 survey conducted by the International Institute for Strategic Studies in London, "With the powerful Pacific Fleet and its land-based naval arm base, these Soviet theatre forces in the Sino-Soviet border area provide a balanced, hard-hitting, and effective force which is trained and equipped for nuclear and for non-nuclear operations."[82]

China also has developed an effective defense force. Chinese communes reacted quickly to Mao's appeal to "dig tunnels deep, store grain everywhere, and accept no hegemony." On the day of my arrival in Peking, July 22, 1976, my wife and I were taken to see an underground shelter. These have been dug in the center of the market and shopping areas. The Director of the Civil Defense Committee told me that such shelters have been built in all major cities. I asked, "Why this huge preparation of underground shelters; from which country does China apprehend aggression?" The reply was clever and unambiguous: "The Soviet social imperialists constitute the main danger." There was no hint of any other external threat, such as one from the United States. Everywhere we went—factories, communes, educational institutions—we were repeatedly told about the dangers from the "Soviet social imperialists."

China has also built a nuclear force to protect itself from Soviet aggression. The latest nuclear test explosions were announced in September and December 1976, in response to the Chinese Communist party's call to turn "grief into strength" over Mao's death. These were China's nineteenth and twentieth blasts since 1964. China has shown restraint as a nuclear power. As Jonathan Pollack of Harvard University pointed out, "Chinese leaders have not been prone to reckless actions nor have they used atomic black-mailings against non-nuclear states. Peking has not transferred nuclear technology or fissionable materials to other countries. . . . Chinese officials have always insisted that their country's 'development of nuclear power is solely for the purpose of self-defence.' The principal objective is to assure that the Chinese acquire an unspecified but survivable retaliatory capability, particularly against the Soviet Union."[83] According to a report by CIA experts on China, "Peking has been cutting back substantially in the last three years (1972-1975) on her expenditures for military equipment."[84] China has not yet begun the development of intercontinental ballistic missiles, which many experts had thought China capable of producing by the mid-1970s, and she has not at this point deployed any sea-launched ballistic missles.

What does China's nuclear program indicate? China is not interested in an expensive arms race with the two superpowers. Nor does China have aspirations of hegemony, being particularly sensitive to the global and security interests of the United States and allies in the Asian-Pacific area. China is basically interested in self-defense against potential Soviet aggression. Like any other nation, it wants to enjoy "freedom from fear." From what I could gather from my talks with Chinese foreign policy makers, experts, party officials, and others, the Soviet Union can no longer afford to launch a preemptive attack on China without major Russian cities, including Moscow, suffering nuclear destruction.

This is a very significant development for the future triangular relationship among Washington, Moscow, and Peking. As we have already pointed out, China responded to Nixon's overtures because of its growing fears of an imminent Russian attack. China is no longer in such a vulnerable position and so does not need U.S. friendship so desperately as it did in 1969-1972. This new factor in China's strategic position will have great significance and impact on Peking's attitude towards Washington and Moscow in the post-Mao period. There are no pro-Moscow or pro-American groups in China: All are pro-China. China will pursue the foreign policy that is perceived to be best suited to China's regional, national, and global interests.

Chapter IV

China and the World

There were no diplomatic relations between China and Japan until 1972, but trade contacts have been extensive since the early 1950s. China's initial hostile attitude toward Japan was a reaction to Japan's separate peace treaty with Taiwan in April 1952, its security treaty with the United States, and its role as a U.S. base during the Korean War. But in September 1954, Chou En-lai told the Chinese National People's Congress that the establishment of normal relations and an expansion of trade with Japan would be of mutual advantage.

Japanese governments began actively to work for closer relations with China. Many unofficial delegations exchanged visits. By 1957, forty-seven so-called "private" contracts, or joint statements, covering such things as trade, fishing, and cultural matters, had been signed. This trade amounted to 2.5 percent of Japan's total overseas trade in 1957.

China suspended trade relations in May 1958, blaming an incident in which a Chinese flag was torn down at a Nagasaki exhibition. Trade decreased enormously. However, after the defeat of Nobosuke Kishi, the Japanese Prime Minister, in July 1960, China became more conciliatory, and Chou En-lai initiated "friendship trade." On the recommendations of the Japan-China Trade Promotion Council (JCTPC), China first traded with a few "friendly" Japanese companies, which pledged to oppose the U.S.-Japan security treaty and to respect Chou's three political "principles": not to adopt a policy inimical to China; not to join a plot to recognize "two Chinas"; and not to hamper attempts to restore normal Sino-Japanese relations. The political qualifications were soon relaxed to increase the number of Japanese trading partners, including "dummy" companies for the Japanese industrial giants, which were conveniently designated as "friendly."

The influence of the Japanese Communist Party (JCP) was extensive in the "friendship trade," exercising great control over the JCTPC. The JCP was often generously financially supported by many of the "friendly" firms.

In late 1962, another form of trade was inaugurated. Chou En-lai and a senior member of Japan's ruling Liberal Democratic Party (LDP), on an unofficial visit to China, agreed to start "memorandum trade" as a way of eventually establishing official economic and political relations. The Liao-Takasaki agreement was signed on September 19, 1962. Unlike friendship trade, memorandum trade contained a semiofficial element, as it was accepted by the leaders of the LDP and was expected to be partly financed by the government-controlled Export-Import Bank.

A memorandum on "over-all" trade was signed for 1963-1967, which provided for two-way trade at about $100 million a year, an exchange of trade liaison personnel, and the application of the method of deferred payment and medium-term credit for China's purchases of Japanese industrial plants. Details were to be negotiated annually in Peking.[85]

Political friction between Peking and Tokyo intensified during 1967. China strongly attacked Japanese Prime Minister Sato, especially over his visits to Taipei and Washington. Also propaganda attacks have been stepped up since Japan signed an agreement with the United States in November 1969 for the return of Okinawa in 1972, in which Japan agreed, "if necessary," to allow military facilities of the United States into both Japan and Okinawa for the defense of South Korea and Taiwan.

The diplomatic agreement between China and Japan, inaugurated by former Prime Minister Tanaka's visit to Peking in September 1972, put an end to the "abnormal state of affairs" between these two important Asian countries. It marked the turning point in their postwar relationship. The links inaugurated by Tanaka's visit in 1972 have been developed by both sides, although the high hopes raised in some quarters in 1972 have not been fulfilled. The 1969 Nixon doctrine, the 1975 Ford Pacific doctrine, the ending of the war in Indo-China, such new Soviet designs as the Brezhnev Asian collective security plan and Russia's bid for preeminence in the Pacific (her Pacific fleet had become a serious challenge to the U.S. Seventh Fleet)—these are some of the factors of the new Asian balance of power, and they constitute weighty reasons for both China and Japan to have good neighborly relations. For the Japanese, China's proximity and size, growing diplomatic stature, and changing relationship with the United States are compelling reasons for rapprochement. Also important are traditional cultural ties, as well as the anticipation of some major economic benefits for Japan from the huge Chinese market.[86] For China, Japan is already its largest trading partner. The Chinese recognize Japan's key role in the changing balance of power in Asia due to its position as the world's third largest economy and her reemergence as a major political power. As one analyst points out, "The American connection with China can have a serious impact on Russia only if the United States also maintains a close rapport with Japan."[87]

The Soviet Union's wooing of Japan is central to its Asian strategy. The recognition in Moscow and Peking that the search for greater influence in Asia entails better relations with Japan was underlined by the prompt arrival of a Chinese ambassador in Tokyo in March 1973 and the quick invitation to Mr. Tanaka to visit Moscow in the same year.

With the opening of diplomatic ties in 1972, China and Japan began to negotiate agreements on civil aviation, navigation, and fisheries. Peking also began to import Japanese steel on a long-term basis, and in the first ten months of 1972 Japan's exports to China ($477.7 million) exceeded those to the Soviet Union ($430.2 million). A governmental agreement, negotiated in the second half of 1973 and signed by Japanese Foreign Minister Orira during a visit to Peking in January 1974, provides for "most favored nation" treatment in tariff and payment arrangements, the establishment of a joint trade committee at the official level, the holding of trade fairs, and the extension of technical exchanges, but the agreement lays down no actual figures. The supplies of Chinese oil to Japan, particularly after the 1973 Arab oil boycott, were mutually beneficial to both countries.[88]

The most serious complicating factor in the Sino-Japanese relationship has been Moscow's bids to acquire influence in Japan. While China has tacitly conceded Japan's need for the security treaty with the United States, she has consistently warned Japan against closer links with the Soviet Union. Like many other Asian countries, Japan wants to maintain a policy of noninvolvement in the Sino-Soviet rift. This has not been easy, as Tokyo has found itself embroiled in the verbal battle between Moscow and Peking.[89] Currently, important issues in the Peking-Tokyo-Moscow diplomacy include the proposed Sino-Japan friendship treaty with its "anti-hegemony" clause. Also significant are the Soviet proposals for Siberian development to be managed jointly with Japan, and for a 2,000-mile second trans-Siberian railway (slightly north of the existing line and in addition to oil pipelines) to convey coal, oil, and other goods to the Pacific coast.

Before I arrived in Peking on July 22, 1976, I spent three days in Tokyo studying the current phase of the Sino-Japanese relationship and the impact on it of the Sino-Soviet feud. I had highly useful discussions at the National Defense College in Tokyo and with some Japanese foreign policy experts. In Peking, I resumed my research on the Peking-Tokyo-Moscow triangle with Chinese foreign policy experts. Let me describe my findings in the two capitals.

Japanese Prime Minister Miki stated in January 1976 that Japan was ready to conclude a peace treaty with China despite Soviet warning against it. Miki's statement was made just hours after Soviet Foreign Minister Gromyko ended a five-day visit to Tokyo.[90] The Soviet Union had expressed strong disapproval of the proposed Sino-Japanese treaty, in which China insists on including a clause against any country's seeking "hegemony" in Asia. Opposition to any form of "hegemony" has become an important feature of China's post-Cultural Revolution foreign policy. This opposition was stated in the 1972 Shanghai communiqué at the close of Nixon's visit to China. It was also expressed in the 1972 Sino-Japanese joint communiqué at the conclusion of Tanaka's visit to Peking, as well as in most of the joint communiqués issued in conjunction with the visits of leaders from other Asian countries to China. In recent months, Japan seems reluctant to include an "anti-hegemony" clause in the treaty with China, as expressed in Miki's statement of January 13, 1976. My Japanese friends cite the following reasons for this reluctance:

1. "Hegemony" has acquired a definite meaning and significance in the Sino-Soviet rift, and Japan would like to remain neutral.

2. China's 1975 constitution speaks against "hegemony of the two superpowers." Japan is not willing to oppose the U.S. presence in Asia, which is vital for her security.

3. If Japan were to sign the treaty with the anti-hegemony clause, Moscow would be so offended that Japan could have no hope of getting back the four northern islands that Russia seized after Japan was defeated in World War II.

When I presented these reasons for Japanese discomfort over the anti-hegemony clause to Chinese foreign policy makers, a senior Chinese expert asked me to tell my Japanese friends, in relation to the Northern islands, that the Russias never return any territory once they occupy it. As for the first reason above, the Chinese told me that the word "hegemony" has a clear and unambiguous meaning; China is opposed to any form of hegemony, not merely the Soviet variety. The Chinese said that Japan is welcome to have special relations with the United States, including security pacts and military bases, but she cannot, as a self-respecting Asian nation, support U.S. hegemony. "Friendship" and "hegemony" are two different things.

Despite the most recent (mid-1976) "cooling off" in the Sino-Japanese relationship and a less than warm relationship between Tokyo and Moscow, China recognizes that Japan's new political and economic strength in Asia will enable her to resist Soviet black-mailing. China is pleased with Tokyo's refusal to be a party to the Brezhnev Asian collective security plan. "A Study of Japan's Defense Issues" by the Japanese Minister of State for Defense in 1975 made the following statements:

> There is a probability that the Soviet Union, its self-confidence buttressed by the Pan-European Security and Cooperation Conference, will strongly advocate the idea of an "Asian Collective Security System" in the near future. This idea has already been proposed by Soviet Communist Party General Secretary Leonid Brezhnev.[91]

> In general, Asian countries have so far remained cool to this idea, primarily due to the many divided nations in this part of the world. Now that Vietnam has been virtually reunified, however, Soviet drives to sell this idea may intensify.
> However events develop in Asia's future, though, the basic Soviet aim is to lure Japan away from China, and increasingly alienate China on the international scene. China, on the other hand, is expected to counter Soviet moves by maneuvering for an advantageous position through friendly relations with the U.S. and Japan.[92]

The *Peking Review* commented in the following way on Soviet designs in Japan:

> The Soviet TASS News Agency issued on June 18, 1975 a "Statement to the Government of Japan," crudely exerting pressure on the Japanese government against including the anti-hegemony clause in the proposed Japan-China treaty of peace and friendship. Thus the Soviet authorities have revealed their hegemonic features.
> The TASS statement attacked China for allegedly "striving to impose by all possible means the inclusion into the treaty of peace and friendship, whose conclusion is being negotiated at the present time, a provision which. . . is aimed, first and foremost, against the Soviet Union."
> However, the wordy statement failed to make clear what provision "is aimed, first and foremost, against the Soviet Union." The Brezhnev clique taboos all mention of "anti-hegemonism" because it is pursuing a policy of hegemonism. Any mention of "opposition to hegemony" throws it into a fit.[93]

> The statement also slanderously accused China of wanting "to involve Japan . . .in the orbit of their foreign policy." Who after all wants to involve Japan in the orbit of his foreign policy? That the Japanese and Chinese governments are negotiating for a Japan-China peace and friendship treaty in accordance with the spirit of the Japan-China statement is a matter concerning only Japan and China. But the Brezhnev clique is so full of rancor against this that it is trying hard to obstruct and undermine the negotiations.[94]

For its part, Japan would probably prefer a better relationship with Peking than with her traditional enemy, the Soviet Union. The Sino-Japanese relationship is based on solid mutual benefits, including feelings of cultural identity.

China and Southeast Asia

China's aim in Southeast and South Asia and throughout the Third World is to secure a major stake in regional affairs at the expense of the Soviet Union—to become both the ideological fountainhead for the world Communist movement and the dominant influence in the developing world.

There have been two major issues in China's relations with the countries of Southeast Asia: (a) Chinese persons abroad, and (b) Peking's alleged support for subversive movements in these countries. China advised Chinese persons abroad to choose local nationalism; those unable to do so have been advised to either respect the law of their adopted land or return to China. This policy was demonstrated in 1966 when Peking repatriated 100,000 Chinese from Indonesia, and in 1969 when it refrained from complaining about the anti-Chinese campaigns in Malaysia. In the post-Cultural Revolution period, China reassured its Southeast Asian neighbors as to the benign nature of its policy toward Chinese abroad. In 1973, it dissolved the Overseas Chinese Affairs Commission, a government body set up in 1969 to watch over 15 million or more overseas Chinese.

China's support for insurgent or "national liberation" movements in Southeast Asia has been a serious hurdle in recent attempts to establish diplomatic relations with the existing regimes of the area, regimes she used to describe as "stooges of American imperialism" or "the feeble-minded bourgeoisie of the East."[95] The Soviet Union has fully exploited regional fears of Chinese support to insurgent movements. For instance, Moscow's *Radio Peace and Progress,* on September 8, 1975, said that Southeast Asian countries face a "common threat to peace from the Chinese-supported insurgent movements," these countries being threatened by armed terrorism. According to the broadcast, "The all-round support given by Peking to the anti-government forces active in Southeast Asian countries is just one of the time bombs planted by Chinese leaders to wreck peace in Asia and to impose their hegemony."

In quest of friendly relations with her Southeast Asian neighbors, China has begun to woo existing regimes and to refuse support of insurgent movements. Peking is anxious to prevent Soviet penetration into the area. The recent establishment of diplomatic relations with Malaysia, The Philippines, and Thailand is indicative of China's preference for establishing government-level links instead of exercising influence through "peoples' diplomacy." It would be naive to think that China will completely stop its support for "national liberation movements" or insurgent movements; at least for the next few years, however, Peking is likely to give priority to diplomatic and friendly relations with her Southeast Asian neighbors. This new policy was adopted by Mao in the post-Cultural Revolution period, and it is most likely to be continued.

China's favorable attitude toward the proposal of ASEAN (Association of Southeast Asian Nations) to establish "a zone of peace, freedom, and neutrality in Southeast Asia," as reaffirmed in the Bali Declaration of February 23-24, 1976, is another indication of China's flexibility.[96] In fact, Peking's recently revised attitude toward ASEAN itself, which it initially described after the August 1967 establishment of the organization as "a new anti-China, anti-Communist alliance," is worth noting. On January 18, 1976, Peking Radio praised the ASEAN nations' efforts at economic cooperation as "successive victories in their common struggle against hegemonism."

The Southeast Asian countries seem no longer to suffer from fears of China's allegedly "exporting revolution." They seem to consider China's new foreign policy objectives as a counterpoise to Soviet advances. Peking is happy to note that none of the Southeast Asian countries endorsed Moscow's "new version of SEATO" (the Brezhnev Asian collective security plan). Peking is worried over the recent Hanoi-Moscow entente but remains confident that the people of Vietnam, who made such great sacrifices to secure their independence, will not be transformed into a satellite, as were the Eastern Europeans after World War II.[97] The Chinese also claim that China and Vietnam are one and have been bound to each other for 2,000 years. To be sure, Vietnam wants independence from China as well as Moscow, but, because of geographical proximity, cultural affinity, and many other factors, the two countries, the Chinese feel, have so much in common that they must stay on good terms.

China and South Asia

After a decade of friendly relations, China and India engaged in a border war in 1962 that resulted in a military debacle for India. Sino-Indian relations were frozen during 1962-1976, and Moscow took full advantage of this. India became Moscow's biggest partner in its policy of isolating and weakening China. India's prime enemy, Pakistan, became China's chief informal ally in South Asia. In November

1970, the Chinese leaders told Pakistan's President Yahya Khan in Peking that India and China might resume the full diplomatic relations which were broken during the 1962 war.[98] But then came the 1971 Bangladesh crisis, and the third Indo-Pakistani war. Both Peking and Washington were unhappy over Moscow's shameless scrambling for power and influence in exploiting regional tensions in South Asia.

As a result of the 1971 crisis, Sino-Indian relations continued to be frozen. Sino-Pakistani ties survived the Chinese Cultural Revolution as well as the Bangladesh crisis and, in fact, became more cordial when Pakistan helped to develop the Sino-American relationship during its formative stages in 1969-1971. The new balance of power that emerged in South Asia after the 1971 crisis was a big diplomatic victory for Moscow, just as it was a setback for China and the United States.[99]

In 1975-1976, the South Asian triangle began to show some changes. India seemed to be getting unhappy over a lack of diplomatic options. During Nehru's heyday, India had enjoyed an excellent diplomatic position: Both the superpowers sought her friendship, and India was a leader of the nonaligned countries. But after the 1971 crisis, her image in the Third World was tarnished; even in Bangladesh, which was her client state during 1972-1974, there was wide anti-Indian feeling culminating in the overthrow of the pro-Indian government on August 15, 1975. More important, India's relations with Washington had not been cordial, and relations with Peking remained frozen. So, India made serious bids to restore full diplomatic relations with Peking.

On April 15, 1975, it was announced that India would send an ambassador to Peking.[100] Though the two countries' ambassadors have presented their credentials in a friendly atmosphere, it is yet too early to forecast substantial links between Peking and New Delhi. India still attaches great importance to Moscow's help, particularly its military supplies, and is not happy over Peking's continued support of Pakistan. Yet, the Indians, as pointed out earlier, want wider diplomatic options. For the Chinese, some dent in the Moscow-New Delhi entente would be a great diplomatic feat. It was reported in the Indian parliament on August 20, 1975 that there had been no anti-Indian propaganda by the Chinese in recent months. Chinese scientists took a week-long study tour of different enterprises and research and development centers in India in October 1976. It was also reported in the Indian parliament that India was exploring prospects for increased trade with China, commerce betweeen the two countries having declined sharply since 1962.[101]

Good neighborly relations between Asia's two largest countries is welcome; they would certainly reduce tensions in South Asia and also would check Moscow's bid for dominance in the subcontinent and the Indian Ocean. The Chinese leaders in the post-Mao period will continue to improve relations with India.

What will be the impact of China's Indian policy on its informal ally in South Asia, Pakistan? Pakistan is, no doubt, worried about prospects of better relations between China and India. I learned from reliable sources in Peking that Islamabad has been assured of China's continued friendship and help, but just as India wants to widen her diplomatic options, so does China want to have more than one friend in South Asia. The present prime minister of Pakistan never tires of talking loudly about his country's links with China. The Chinese know, however, that it was Mr. Bhutto who turned down Chou En-lai's offer of a "Friendship Pact" on January 27, 1964.[102] Similarly, when President Ayub was reshaping Pakistan's foreign policy after the 1962 Sino-Indian war and trying to improve relations with Peking, Mr. Bhutto's advice to Ayub was "to look toward Moscow" instead of Peking.

In an important note on April 6, 1969, Ayub wrote Bhutto: "You are trying to drag me into a futile venture. The Russians won't be our friends because of their long-standing commitments to India and Afghanistan. If the Soviets wish to improve relations with us, they could have done so in many ways. At present, they will wish only to play with us."[103] Pakistan recognized the wisdom of this warning in 1971 when the Soviet Union backed India in the dismemberment of Pakistan. The Chinese will continue to have friendly relations with Pakistan, because they know that the people and the army of Pakistan, not Bhutto, are the solid core of Pakistan's close ties with Peking.

China began diplomatic relations with the new South Asian nation, Bangladesh, after the military coup there on August 15, 1975. Earlier, Bangladesh under Mujib, the founder of the country, adopted a negative attitude toward Peking under the joint influence of India and the Soviet Union. With the change in the Bangladesh government in August 1976, China extended her full support and cooperation to Bangladesh. The new relationship is still in its formative phase, but both sides are eager to develop it quickly and in mutual interest. Bangladesh is likely to provide another foothold for China in the Indian subcontinent-Indian Ocean area.

China and Africa

China has been working hard to extend her influence among developing nations, particularly in Africa. In the early 1960s China predicted that revolutionary prospects were excellent in Africa. According to Premier Chou En-lai, the essence of Maoism is the idea of the party combining its leadership with a spontaneous broad mass movement to bring about a "continuing revolution." In line with this theory, the Chinese, unlike the Russians, have concentrated on the backward elements in society rather than on trying to win over an emerging intelligentsia.

On a world scale, the countries of Asia, Africa, and Latin America, which in their immediately postcolonial period can be said to be suffering abnormal conditions of insecurity and stress, are, in the Chinese view, ideal ground for their theories. They have therefore paid special attention to Africa, which they consider occupies an important position in the "countryside of the world." The situation in southern Africa, where the majority of countries have been under metropolitan or white minority governments, presents the Chinese with the opportunity to exploit conditions of extreme stress, but they do not confine their hopes of violent revolution to these areas. They have exploited rebellion against independent African governments which they regard as bourgeois, as in the case of Zaire (formerly Congo-Kinshasa).

The assessment by Chou En-lai that Africa was ripe for revolution was not liked by the African states, just as China's Asian neighbors did not like its support of insurgent movements in Asia. In the post-Cultural Revolution period, China has changed her technique. She is now more interested in establishing diplomatic relations than in promoting revolution in Africa. Four main objectives seem to govern China's new diplomatic strategy in Africa: (a) the reestablishment of China as a world power; (b) the expansion of foreign trade with China; (c) the curtailment of Soviet power in the world Communist movement; and (d) the erosion of the influence of Western colonial powers.

Chinese interest in Africa became apparent in 1955 with the first Afro-Asian conference in Bandung. Addressing the National People's Congress (NPC) in Peking on May 13, 1955, Chou En-lai stated that "the Asian-African conference inspired all oppressed nations and peoples in Asia, Africa, Latin-America, and other parts of the world in their fight for independence and freedom."[104] China repeatedly drew attention to the relevance of her revolutionary experiences and, in the absence of the Russians at the conference, seized the chance to develop a new sphere of influence among African nations moving toward independence. They quickly established diplomatic and other relations with Ghana and Guinea, which were among the first African states to become independent.

At this point, Soviet and Chinese objectives coincided, in that both nations were working to reduce Western influence in the world. With the outbreak of the Sino-Soviet dispute, however, the Chinese revived an idea, first put forward by Mao in 1946, of two distinct worlds opposed to both superpowers (i.e., opposed to the Soviet Union *and* the United States). In the Chinese view, there are three worlds in existence today. The first is that of the superpowers, which are contending for global control. The Second World consists of the developed countries of Western Europe, Japan, Australia, and Canada. Allied with the second is the Third World, consisting of the developing countries of Asia, Africa, and Latin America. China considers herself a member of the Third World, though she is an emerging superpower in terms of population, territory, and military power. She aspires to leadership of the combined Second and Third worlds.

Africa has been affected by the Sino-Soviet dispute in three main ways. First the Chinese have challenged the Russians in the international Communist front organizations and in the Afro-Asian People's Solidarity Organization (AAPSO), causing splits in existing bodies and setting up new, Chinese-sponsored ones. Second, the national liberation movements have been weakened, with the two Communist powers backing rival bodies from the same territory. The emergence of a pro-Soviet and pro-Chinese wings has also occurred in some "revolutionary" political parties, among them the *Union des Populations du Cameroun* (UPC) and the *Parti Africain de l' Independence* in Senegal, as well as in some of the liberation movements. Finally, the propaganda war has affected Africans, over whose heads it has often been fought.

The Sino-Soviet dispute directly affected attempts to hold a second Afro-Asian conference (a successor to the Bandung Conference) in Algiers in June 1965. This meeting was seen by the Chinese as a counterbalance to the Second Non-Aligned Conference held in Cairo in October 1964, which they did not attend. One of the objects of Chou En-lai's tour of Africa in early 1964 was to stir up support for the Afro-Asian conference. A preparatory meeting for the conference, in April 1964 in Djakarta, discussed whether or not the Soviet Union should be invited. The Chinese maintained that the Soviet Union should be excluded, on the grounds that it was neither an African nor an Asian country. The Soviet government challenged this, and the debate continued throughout the year. On June 19, 1965, the Algerian President, Ben Bella, was overthrown in a military coup, and the Chinese immediately recognized his successor, Colonel Houari Boumediene, in their concern that the conference should go ahead. Nevertheless, it was postponed until November; and, by September, the Chinese foreign minister, Chen Yi, indicated a diminution of interest, since Soviet participation was still not excluded. On November 2, a meeting of foreign ministers decided that the conference should be abandoned indefinitely, in view of the differences between members.[105]

The propaganda war in Africa between the Chinese and the Russians continues sporadically, mainly in the form of reciprocal attacks on ideology, aid projects, and conferences sponsored by either side. Lately, the Russians have been the more active. In July and September 1970, they hit at Chinese economic, political, and diplomatic activities in Africa and have since accused Peking of splitting the unity of the African liberation movement.

While the Chinese are unlikely to withhold criticism of the Soviet Union entirely, they may now moderate their attacks so as not to damage the image, which they are now endeavoring to establish, of a responsible international power. But the basic ideological differences between the Russians and the Chinese remain unresolved, and competition to increase their influence in the developing world is becoming keener.

Clearly a component of China's more outward-looking foreign policy is her renewed effort to assume leadership of the liberation struggle in Africa, displacing the Soviet Union's predominating influence in the principal freedom movements. However, China faces a dilemma in supporting dissident groups inside countries with which she is pursuing normal diplomatic relations. There are signs of increasing caution in China's dealing with such groups, and most likely the Chinese will concentrate their attention on liberation movements that operate in areas where they have no diplomatic or economic relations to compromise.

Announcing on June 11, 1971 that his government had recognized China, Libya's President Quadhafi pointed to its growing importance as a world power—emphasizing that his government's decision was a realistic and political one that owed nothing to

Peking's ideological claims. As a country on which atheism had been imposed, China was a stranger, he said. Chinese influence would never be allowed to spread in Libya.[106]

Quadhafi's view is shared by many Middle Eastern and African leaders, who are prepared to recognize China (in part, to balance Soviet overtures) and to trade with it but would resist any attempt by China to influence their social and political systems. Peking is taking more account of these sensibilities than in the early 1960s, when Chou En-lai proclaimed that Africa was ripe for revolution. At present, China's increased activity in Africa is concentrated mainly in the diplomatic and economic spheres. Relations recently have been established with Nigeria, Cameroon, Equatorial Guinea, Ethiopia, and Kuwait, and, through economic, technical, and medical cooperation, Peking is trying to show that she understands, better than Moscow does, the needs of the developing world.

Peking's aid to Africa (but not the Middle East) now exceeds Moscow's. Personnel from the Chinese army first went to Tanzania in 1964, initially for a six-month stay, to assist in training police, army, and navy cadets. They subsequently became involved in training exiled Congolese and other rebel guerrillas. The Chinese have become the sole instructors of the Tanzanian armed forces—a logical development, according to President Nyerere, as the army uses mainly Chinese weapons. The other major African recipient of Chinese military aid is Zaire.[107] The 1972 visits by Chinese military delegations to Guinea and Mali may presage attempts to secure an important role in their armies too. China's aid program has an outstanding reputation for rapid implementation, good terms, and lack of political strings, but it is still too small to make a major impact. Much goodwill was won by the completion of the 1,250-mile, f170 million (U.S. $30 million) Tanzania-Zambia railway, ahead of schedule, but such massive undertakings are by no means typical.

Focus on Portuguese colonies

Chinese diplomatic effort in Africa in the early 1970s was concentrated on the Portuguese territories. The Chinese are particularly interested in Mozambique, which they clearly regard as an important element in the struggle for southern Africa. Chinese influence in FRELIMO, the only Mozambique party to be recognized by the Organization for African Unity (OAU), was at a low ebb for a period following the 1970 expulsion from leadership of the pro-Chinese

Uria Simango, after a prolonged period of rivalry between pro-China and pro-Soviet factions. But the turning point came in August 1971 when a FRELIMO delegation, led by the movement's President, Samora Marchel, spent six weeks touring China, North Korea, and North Vietnam.

As well as challenging the Soviet grip on FRELIMO, the Chinese have cultivated a number of Mozambiquan break-away minority groups. Much of their support was given to the Mozambique Revolutionary Committee (COREMO), formed by dissidents from FRELIMO and led by Paulo Gumane. COREMO has received financial aid from the Chinese, who have also agreed to supply arms provided that these are sent through channels other than those of the OAU Liberation Committee. (The Committee has previously confiscated arms intended for COREMO, which it does not recognize.) The Chinese also offered guerrilla training, and by the end of 1971 a group including three members of the COREMO Central Committee had returned from a three-month course in China. Chinese training of African guerrillas has been a source of worry to the African states.[108]

A split in COREMO itself led to the formation of a further splinter group, ULIPAMO, which also receives Chinese assistance. Another small group, PAPOMO, is known to have been given funds by the Chinese in an attempt to build up a Mozambique Communist party, the nucleus of which had previously existed secretly.

In spite of their involvement in smaller movements, the Chinese have continued to give substantial military aid to FRELIMO. The movement is now believed to be mainly equipped by the Chinese, who have provided modern weapons (such as assault guns, antitank launchers, and projectiles), unloaded from Chinese ships at Dar es Salaam and Mtwara.[109]

Chinese military experts have also been reported fighting alongside guerrillas in both Mozambique and in Angola. There, the Chinese have stepped up attempts to influence the MPLA, a traditionally Soviet-sponsored movement in which efforts to set up a pro-Chinese faction have failed in the past. As in FRELIMO's case, new Chinese initiatives towards MPLA can be traced back to mid-1971. In August, an MPLA delegation, led by its President, Agostinho Neto, visited Peking at the invitation of the Chinese-African Friendship Association. The delegation also visited North Vietnam and North Korea. Since then, MPLA freedom fighters have received Chinese training.

The second half of 1971, therefore, saw a reactivation and reorganization of China's involvement in the liberation struggle in southern Africa. China had not only increased the level of its assistance but also extended it to those parties previously connected mainly with the Russians, including smaller movements such as the South West African People's Organization (SWAPO) and the Liberation Committee of Sao Tome and Principe (CLSTP). In redesigning its aid program, China appeared to be concentrating on those areas where freedom fighters have had some success.

China was the only Communist party to give direct assistance, including arms, to the secessionist Eritrean Liberation Front (also ELF) in Ethiopia. In June 1969, an ELF official confirmed that two shiploads of Chinese arms had been purchased during that year. Guerrillas have also been trained in China (20 were selected in 1967) and supplied with uniforms and equipment. However, one of the Front's leaders, Omar Jaber, admitted on November 2, that China no longer offered support, adding that "this may be explained by the policy of China to widen its international relations."[110]

On March 18, 1976, China accused the Soviet Union in the Security Council of "hatching new schemes" in southern Africa in the wake of its armed intervention in Angola. The Soviet representative dismissed the charge as "nonsense" and asserted that China had become a friend of the "racists in South Africa" and of "imperialist circles that had wanted to block the struggle for independence in Angola."[111]

These particular acrimonious exchanges between Chinese and Soviet delegates—which have become commonplace in the United Nations—occurred during a debate of a resolution calling for international assistance to Mozambique. The text advocated economic aid for Mozambique so as to enable it to maintain the sanctions against Rhodesia that it had initiated earlier that month. The resolution was adopted unanimously.

China's chief delegate, Huang Hua, said that the "Soviet social-imperialists" were attempting "to interfere in and undermine the national liberation movement in Southern Africa." Mikhail A. Kharlamov of the Soviet Union said that his government had not intervened in Angola but had been "on the side of the forces of progress," helping the Angolan people to strengthen their independence. The Soviet representative stated that, under agreements signed last month, Moscow was already giving "material assistance" to Mozambique.

In rejoinder, the Chinese delegate referred to "the crimes" that he said the Soviet Union had committed in Angola to further its design of "colonial expansion" and world hegemony. The Soviet

representative said the Chinese tirades had "bored everybody."[112]
Commenting on the Soviet role and designs in Africa, Premier
Hua Kuo-feng (now Chairman Hua) said on July 16, 1976,

> The situation in Africa is most heartening. The great African people are
> engaged in united struggle against imperialism, colonialism, neocolonialism, big-
> power hegemonism, white racism, and Zionism and are advancing in big strides.
> Particularly noteworthy at present is the fact that, while one superpower is
> bolstering the racist regimes in various ways in order to preserve its vested interests
> in southern Africa, the other superpower which claims to be the "natural ally" of
> the African people is carrying out in a more cunning way its expansion and infil-
> tration in southern Africa under the signboard of "supporting" the national-
> liberation movements, its purpose being to gain control of the strategically impor-
> tant southern Africa. The tasks of struggle for the African people remain arduous.
> But we are deeply convinced that neither the racists' last-gasp struggle nor super-
> power interference and sabotage can stop the African people from marching for-
> ward. The great African people, heightening their vigilance, strengthening their
> unity, and persisting in struggle, will surely win the complete independence and
> liberation of the entire African continent. The Chinese government and people
> will, as always, stand on the side of the African people and firmly support their
> just struggle.[113]

China and the Middle East and Mediterranean

China's relations with the Arab world, unlike those of the Soviet
Union, have not been hampered by diplomatic ties with Israel,
although Israel recognized China in 1949—the first Middle East
country to do so. (The Soviet Union did not break off diplomatic
relations with Israel until after the Middle East war in June 1967.)
China's relative freedom from involvement with established governments, plus its nonmembership in the UN until 1971, have allowed it
to adopt a flexible Mideast policy.

The undermining of Western influence was a primary aim of
China's activity in the Middle East, but the escalation of the Sino-
Soviet dispute has caused China to give increasing priority to attacks
on Soviet influence and its role in the Middle East.

China has made use of its greater freedom of movement chiefly
in its support of the Palestine liberation organizations, contrasting a
"people's war" interpretation of the Arab-Israel dispute with the
Soviet's search for a political solution. In his Middle East visit in
1963-1964, Chou En-lai pointed out that China had "supported the
people of Palestine in their struggle for national sovereignty and re-
gaining their lost homeland" since the 1955 Bandung conference. At
Bandung, Chou had made the first clear statement of what remains

China's interpretation of the creation of Israel: that it was the result of "American imperialist intervention" and that it is a "tool of U.S. imperialism."

The Chinese stand on the Arab cause in the Middle East was repeatedly expressed in the 1950s and 1960s by Chinese leaders and by the Chinese press. Whether on the Suez Canal question or on Syria's fight for safeguarding national independence, or on any other struggle of the Arab people against colonialism, China has consistently stood on the side of the Arab people.[114] About the Suez crisis, Mao said, "We firmly support the entirely lawful action of the Government of Egypt in taking back the Suez Canal Company and resolutely oppose any attempt to encroach on the sovereinty of Egypt and start armed intervention against that country. We must completely frustrate the schemes of imperialism to create tension and prepare for war."[115]

Lin Shao-chi, commenting on the Suez crisis, also gave full support to Egypt: "The struggle between the aggressive policy of imperialism and the anti-aggression movement of nationally independent states is being intensified in the Middle East. Egypt has widespread sympathy all over the world. . . . The policy of armed intervention on the question of the Suez Canal, and indeed on all other questions relating to the national independence movements, can only result in utter failure."[116]

After the promising start of China's relations with the United Arab Republic, Chinese "extremism" and increased Soviet economic aid placed President Nasser effectively on the Soviet side in the Sino-Soviet dispute. After the 1967 war, China made an attempt to exploit disillusion with the Soviet Union by offering the United Arab Republic wheat and money but withdrew the offer after the Khartoum conference made it clear that Egypt would not be won over to the Chinese line on Israel.

The internal difficulties of the Cultural Revolution prevented China from fully exploiting disillusion with the Soviet Union after the 1967 war and developing relations with countries, such as Syria, Algeria, and Iraq, which agree with China about leaving the Arab-Israeli dispute to the Palestinian guerrillas. At the same time, the role of some Chinese radicals in Arab countries during the Cultural Revolution led to difficulties with, for example, Morocco and to a break in diplomatic relations with Tunisia.

Thus, although China maintains diplomatic relations with countries in the area, her greatest impact has been in her influence on such movements as the Dhofar Liberation Front and, above all, the Palestinian guerrilla organizations. The Palestinian Liberation Organization (PLO) was set up after the January 1964 Arab summit, and a PLO office was opened in Peking after a visit to China in March 1965 by the PLO General-Secretary, Ahmed Shuqairy. The PLO lost influence after June 1967, and nothing was heard of the Peking office after Shuqairy's dismissal in December of that year, until it was announced, in July 1969, that a new head had been appointed to the office.

However, China has continued to give training and some arms to other movements, such as al-Fatah, and her ideological influence on the more extreme groups, notably the Popular Democratic Front for the Liberation of Palestine, has been considerable.

At the same time, there have been recent signs that China is interested in a gradual extension of more conventional relations with Algeria, Iraq, Syria, and other Arab countries. President Anwar Sadat's abrogation of the friendship treaty with Moscow, on March 15, 1976, gave Peking an excellent opportunity to step into Middle Eastern affairs through association with this influential Arab country. Chiao Kuan-hua, in a speech to the UN General Assembly, demonstrates the way China was able to associate itself with Egypt, against the Soviet Union: "The heroic people of Egypt, unable to bear social-imperialist bullying and oppression any longer, resolutely abrogated the Egyptian-Soviet treaty."[117]

After blasting the Soviets' crude diplomacy in dealings with smaller nations, President Sadat approached both Indian and China in October 1975 with requests for much-needed military spare parts which the Soviet Union had refused to supply. Both India and China manufacture Soviet-type equipment. India turned down the Egyptian request because of a Soviet veto, but China provided thirty engines for MIG 17 and MIG 21 fighter-bombers as a "gift." Relations between Peking and Cairo grew warmer. Egyptian Vice-President Mubarek arrived in Peking for a visit on April 20, 1976, and a Chinese-Egyptian military protocol was signed the next day.[118] The signing of the pact highlighted a series of 1976 successes for Peking in its diplomatic rivalry with Moscow. We might note that in 1976, the newly-elected prime ministers of Australia and New Zealand came to Peking and expressed grave concerns about Soviet naval expansion in the Indian Ocean.

During my three-day stay in Cairo in July 1976, enroute to Peking, I had lengthy talks with the Chinese ambassador in Cairo (an old friend of mine) and with some senior Egyptian foreign ministry officials. Both China and Egypt seem eager to develop closer relations. Having been unhappy over Moscow's growing influence in the Middle East during the mid-1950s and 1960s, Peking is delighted to develop friendly relations with Middle Eastern countries. While the Soviet Union has stepped up its propaganda campaign against China's claims of friendship and support for Arab peoples, Peking's reply is a recitation of her record of unqualified support for the Arabs at the United Nations and in other international forums. The Palestine Liberation Organization has been given full diplomatic recognition by Peking, and, since China entered the UN in 1971, the Chinese delegation has never failed to give unqualified support to the Arabs on the Middle East issue. Let us refer to some of the speeches of the chief of the Chinese UN delegation on the Middle East.

The present situation of "no war, no peace" in the Middle East is solely created by the two superpowers for their respective interests. Taking advantage of this situation, they are using Arab countries' territories and sovereignty and the Palestinian people's right to existence as stakes to strike political deals. The United States is openly supporting the aggression by Israeli Zionism. The other superpower claims to "support and assist" the Arab people in their struggle against aggression. Has it supported and assisted them? It has indeed sold them no small amount of weapons. But strangely, the weapons supplied are not allowed to be used. Is this not asking people to buy scrap iron? Moreover, it demands privileges and bases, and even attempts to subvert their government. What kind of "friend" is this? It is more dangerous than an open enemy.[119]

Although the two superpowers are both trumpeting about a general world trend towards detente, a tense stalemate of "no war, no peace" still prevails in the Middle East. When the Soviet Union dismembered Pakistan in 1971, no one said there was a risk of a nuclear war. Neither has anyone made a similar warning in connection with the current U.S. intervention in Cambodia. It is only in connection with the Middle East that, at the mention by Arab countries to repulse Israeli aggression and recover their lost territories, the air is filled with cries about the risk of a nuclear war between the two superpowers. Why is this so? Because the situation of "no war, no peace" created and maintained by the two superpowers serves them best in their scramble for spheres of influence, oil resources, and strategic positions in the Middle East. China firmly supports the Palestinian and other Arab peoples in their just struggle against Israeli Zionism. We believe that, so long as they uphold unity and preserve their struggle, the Palestinian and other Arab peoples, with the support of the people of the whole world, will certainly surmount all the difficulties on their road of advancement, recover their sacred territories, and regain their national rights.[120]

The Arab people brought about an excellent situation through fighting the October War. This war has strengthened the confidence of the Arab people in victory over the Israeli aggressor and broken the stalemate that was deliberately created by the superpowers. Now, a disengagement has been affected between Egypt and Israel and between Syria and Israel, but the Middle East question is still far from being settled.

> The essence of the Middle East question lies in Israeli Zionist aggression and the contention between the two superpowers, the United States and the Soviet Union, for hegemony in the Middle East, versus the struggle of the Palestinian and other Arab peoples against aggression and hegemonism.
>
> The Chinese government and people always support the just struggle of the Palestinian and other Arab peoples. From the very beginning, we have refused to have any contact with the Israeli Zionists who persist in aggression. We have firmly opposed the contention between the two superpowers in the Middle East and opposed their support to, and connivance with, Israel, and constantly exposed the truth that social-imperialism is giving sham support while attempting to control the Palestinian and other Arab peoples.
>
> Restoration of Palestinian national rights and recovery of the lost Arab territories form an integral struggle. There can be no settlement of the Middle East question so long as the lost Arab territories are not recovered and Palestinian national rights not restored.[121]

The Mediterranean area, along with Europe and the Middle East, is now a prime focus of contention between the two superpowers— and thus a field where Chinese diplomatic activities can oppose the "hegemony" of superpowers (or, what really concerns Peking, "Soviet social imperialism"). A country such as Algeria is a natural focus for Chinese overtures based on Third World "solidarity." However, the area still seems to be a low priority in China's current strategy, although the Chinese clearly recognize the strategic importance for the major naval powers of facilities in the Mediterranean—a factor that presumably accounts for their attention to Malta and Cyprus.

China and Iran

China watches with concern the Soviet naval expansion in the Indian Ocean, welcoming Iran's growing military strength. Iran and China boast of a friendship that has lasted for 3,000 years. The two countries were known to have been linked through the ancient silk route.

Iran and China established diplomatic relations on August 17, 1971. During my stay in Peking in July-August 1976, the Shah of Iran's sister, Princess Ashraf, was there, and my hosts were full of praise for the Shah. The Shah's efforts to bring about a rapprochement between Pakistan and India, and Pakistan and Afghanistan, are highly appreciated by the Chinese, as such rapprochement will reduce Moscow's influence in both India and Afghanistan. The official New China News Agency (NCNA), in a commentary in September 1976, supported Iran's military build-up with U.S. weapons and criticized Moscow for its disapproval of Iran's arms purchases. The commentary said, "As an independent sovereign state, Iran has the right and every reason to ensure her self-defense. As to the kinds and number of weapons it intends to buy and from where it buys them it is the internal affair of Iran, and other countries have no right to intervene. Must Iran explain her justification to the Kremlin when exercising her sovereignty?"[122]

China and Western Europe

In recent years, China has taken an active interest in West European affairs. Only five years ago, China denounced the European Economic Community (EEC) as a "center of imperialist contradictions" and an "American Machine." Then in 1975, China became the second communist country (after Yugoslavia) to open official relations with the EEC. Peking's preoccupation with the Soviet threat has led it to favor a stronger, united Western Europe. It has spoken favorably about NATO as a counterbalance to the increasing Soviet military strength in Europe.

Peking has reasons to be satisfied with the responses it has received from the West European leaders. British Prime Minister Heath, French President Pompidou, German Chancellor Helmut Schmitt, and Belgium Premier Leo Tindenmans have all visited China during the last three or four years. China now has diplomatic relations with all Western European countries except Ireland.

In May 1975, the visits of the EEC Commissioner for External Affairs, Sir Christopher Soames, to Peking and of Chinese Vice-Premier Teng Hsiao-ping to Paris once again underlined China's interest in West European affairs. Teng, during his stay in Paris, praised the movement towards West European unity as "a means of safeguarding its members' independence and security." The Chinese are evidently convinced that there is a need for keeping a united front with countries of all political persuasions to counter the threat from the two superpowers, and particularly from the ambitions of the Soviet Union.

The alleged Soviet threat takes precedence over all other considerations in China's approach to the different European states, though the importance of these countries as a source of advanced technology and capital equipment is not forgotten while China is unable to provide these adequately for herself. The Chinese leaders have referred to Europe, together with the Mediterranean and the Middle East, as the main focus of contention between the superpowers; references to an imminent Soviet attack on their own country have been replaced by talk of a "feint to the East" designed to mask an "attack in the West." Besides supporting the EEC and any widening of its membership, they have spoken favorably in private of the North Atlantic Treaty Organization (NATO) and the Western alliance. They have tended to show a preference for those Western governments and politicians most wary of the Soviet Union and have been cool towards Social Democratic leaders such as Herr Brandt, whose Ostpolitik they regarded as a dangerous flirtation with the Soviet bloc. After it recognized Peking in 1964, France was the target of the warmest Chinese overtures, until its growing friendship with the Soviet Union in the late 1960s clouded its Chinese friendship. It has since returned to the forefront of China's attention in Western Europe.

During Sir Christopher Soames' visit, the first by a top EEC official, Premier Chou En-lai and his colleagues made much of the importance China attached to a united Europe, according to delegation sources. On his way home, Sir Christopher told journalists in Hong Kong, on May 12, 1975, that the Chinese wanted to see Europe "as strong as it can be in an economic and political sense."[123] He said that China would be sending an ambassador to the EEC headquarters in Brussels at a later date and would give "positive consideration" to the conclusion of a trade agreement with the Community. A joint commission of Chinese and EEC trade officials, he said, would also be discussed when further talks were held in Brussels. By contrast, neither the Soviet Union nor any of its fellow members in the Soviet-led Council for Mutual Economic Assistance (CMEA) have so far established formal relations with the EEC—which is, of course, another reason why the Chinese wish to do so.

Peking has also shown an interest in the expansion of ties between the EEC and the developing world. At a farewell banquet for Sir Christopher on May 8, Li Chiang, the Minister of Foreign Trade, said that, if all countries "subjected to superpower aggression, interference, and control" united, they would be able to frustrate superpower schemes for "world hegemony."[124] Two months earlier, the New China News Agency had hailed the Lome Convention between the EEC and forty-six African, Caribbean, and Pacific developing states as a "big event in the development of relations between the Second and Third World countries," which should aid the worldwide struggle "against the superpowers and their hegemonistic practices." The recent improvement in France's relationship with Algeria has no doubt also caused satisfaction in Peking.

When France established full relations with Peking in 1964, President de Gaulle was in power, and his independent policy with regard to NATO and the United States was probably noted with favor by the Chinese. The picture changed as France moved towards closer ties with the Soviet Union. But President Pompidou's visit in September 1973, the first to Communist China by a West European head of state, reaffirmed France's importance to Peking. Teng Hsiao-ping, who returned President Pompidou's visit with his trip to France on May 12-17, is the highest-ranking Chinese leader to visit Western Europe. (A vice-chairman of the Communist party, as well as vice-premier, Teng was the leader with most seniority fit to travel.) It was announced during his stay that France and China would hold regular discussions at the foreign minister level—a new departure in China's relations with Western Europe—and that a joint commission would be set up to promote economic exchanges.[125] (Nevertheless, in terms of trade with Peking, France comes well behind the German Federal Republic.)

In June 1976, the Chief of the French General Staff, General Guy Mery, was the first, and so far the only, Western chief-of-staff, to inspect Chinese military installations—and meet all the right people-during his ten-day visit. Now President Valéry Giscard d'Estaing wants to be the next head-of-state to visit China.

Franco-Chinese relations were somewhat distant while Georges Pompidou was President but have improved since Giscard d'Estaing has taken over, especially during 1976. President d'Estaing has strengthened France's relations with the Atlantic Alliance, despite strong opposition from the Gaullists and the powerful French Left, which has a good chance of winning the parliamentary elections in 1978. He has established good relations with the United States and is working for the economic, political, and diplomatic unity of the European community. In addition, d'Estaing is more hesitant than was General de Gaulle and President Pompidou in accepting Soviet assurances on detente at their face value and agrees with Peking that Moscow is trying to encircle and isolate China.

While diplomatic relations between Paris and Peking were flourishing in 1976, trade relations were extremely modest. No major contracts were signed or are in the process of negotiation. On the contrary, Sino-French trade has been practically at a standstill since May 1976.

Rumors that General Mery went to Peking not only on a good will tour but also to sell French military hardware—particularly the amphibious AMX-30 tank—have been vigorously denied by French officials and industry.

Politically, the Chinese are giving full support to the present French government. Although Peking has lately adopted a more open attitude toward European communism and has discreetly started to improve relations with the Italian Communist party, the Chinese have not changed their hostile attitude toward the French Communist party, nor is there any indication that they intend to do so in the foreseeable future.

With the approach of the Common Market referendum, Chinese comment stressed the wide support in Britain for continued membership and ignored the opposition from both Right and Left. In a long report on April 11 about the House of Commons debate on the subject, the NCNA quoted only those speakers who recommended continued membership.

China's press and radio have taken a close interest in European defense matters. Without openly endorsing the Western alliance, its leaders have told visiting Western politicians of their approval of NATO's existence and of the role it can play as a counter to "aggressive" Soviet designs. The Chinese draw favorable attention to moves to strengthen the Western armed forces and are generally critical of defense cuts. Noting a build-up of Warsaw Pact forces in March, for instance, an NCNA commentary quoted criticisms of British cuts in defense expenditures. Both the Conference on Security and Cooperation in Europe (CSCE) and the talks in Vienna on Mutual and Balanced Force Reductions (MFR) have been dismissed by Chinese sources as futile in the light of Moscow's real aims.

In recent years, the West European countries have benefited in their exports to China from its need to acquire sophisticated goods and equipment which cannot be manufactured easily at home: Their exports have generally been growing faster than their imports from China. They have also increased their share of China's total foreign trade. Figures for 1973 show that trade with Western Europe accounted for nearly 20 percent of China's total foreign trade and that the original six EEC states accounted for four-fifths of this figure. In 1974, the expanded Community became China's third largest trading partner (behind Japan and Hong Kong).

The German Federal Republic is predominant in China's exchanges with Western Europe, with a turnover each year nearly double that of other EEC states. Britain, France, and Italy rank next in importance. These countries will consolidate their position as China's leading West European trading partners as the goods and equipment already contracted for are delivered. Recent contracts concluded by West European firms with China involve the sale of a total of 30 British Trident aircraft, with deliveries extending into 1976, a $264 million (£110 million) steel-making complex for Wuhan, to be constructed by a West German consortium and operational by 1977, and $1 billion (£416 million) worth of orders from French firms for transport equipment and petrochemical plants.

Chapter V

Post-Mao China and the World

Which way China? This question was raised by the recent death of Chairman Mao Tse-tung, long the ultimate decision maker on China's vital issues, and of Chou En-lai, who was China's ablest administrator, particularly in the realm of external affairs. The Peoples' Republic of China is a nation of nearly a billion people and is equipped with nuclear weapons—not yet a superpower but with the potential to become one. Already a major power, it is destined to play a central role in world affairs. China's international role after Mao and Chou has, therefore, great significance.

What will be the future trends in the Sino-American relationship? Will the Sino-Soviet rift, to which Mao was a major contributor, continue, or will there be a closing of differences, a development that would affect not only the two giants but also the fragile triangular relationship between Washington, Moscow, and Peking? Will there be any major change in the balance of power in the Asian-Pacific region where the interests of all major powers interact? What will be the relationship between the global competition of major powers and the regional tensions and conflicts in the Middle East, southern Africa, and in many parts of the Third World, where the big powers have been carrying on multifaced war by proxy, as in Angola? Will there be chaos and confusion in China after Mao? What is the significance of the so-called power struggle in China, or, rather, what is the true meaning of the debate between the two schools of Chinese thought that led many China experts in this country and elsewhere to make gloomy forecasts about what might happen after Mao's death? Let me describe the Chinese political scene I witnessed in July 1976, before Mao's death.

Some groups in the United States and elsewhere believe China is on the verge of a great political upheaval. The death of Chou En-lai, the subsequent dismissal of Teng Hsiao-ping, the riots at Tien An Men Square on April 5, 1976, and finally the death of Chairman Mao are responsible for such forecasts about China. The Cultural Revolution of 1966-1968 evoked other pessimistic forecasts about China. But from my vantage point as Director-General in the Pakistan Foreign Ministry, I gained a different impression. In spite of the alleged "widespread dislocation" and "destruction" resulting from the Cultural Revolution, Pakistan received regular shipments of arms from China strictly on schedule. During the same period, the Chinese established a new ordnance factory at Dacca (then capital of East Pakistan, now capital of Bangladesh).

When I arrived in Hong Kong from China on August 1, 1976, journalists attempted to confirm the "great panic, confusion, and chaos in Peking" caused by the severe earthquake that had taken place on July 26. My impression was that the Chinese people in Peking and the surrounding area showed a strong sense of discipline and displayed no signs of panic.

These incidents suggest that the gloomy forecasts by "China experts" of political upheaval may be premature; their suggestions that the United States should "wait and watch" before making any further step toward improving Sino-American relations may be doing a great disservice to America's vital global interests. One must keep in mind that the Soviet leaders would like to destroy the emerging Sino-American relationship.

The future of China after Chairman Mao's death is a crucial question about which no one can make absolutely sure predictions. As Chairman Hua has said, "While our people, our comrades, and our foreign friends and comrades were gnawed by deep anxiety and concern over the destiny of our party and state, everybody was saying to himself: In the past with Chairman Mao at the helm, we defied whatever difficulty or hazard was before us; now that Chairman Mao has passed away, what will become of China's future?"[126] Then Hua, of course, confidently stated, "Filled with the pride of victory, the Chinese people declare to the whole world: We have stood the severe test. Under the guidance of Chairman Mao's revolutionary line, our party has won, the proletariat has won, the people have won, the bright socialist China has won!"[127]

Yet one can make some projections of the likely trends in China's domestic and international behavior in the post-Mao period. The Chinese themselves conclude that "class contradictions, the class struggle between the proletariat and the bourgeoisie, and the struggle between the socialist road and the capitalist road exist throughout the transitional period. We shall go astray if we forget this fundamental theory and practice of our party over the last dozen years or so."[128] The new Chinese constitution, as adopted at the Fourth National People's Congress on January 17, 1975, clearly states, "Socialist society covers a considerably long historical period. Throughout this historical period, there are class contradictions and class struggles; there is the struggle between the socialist road and the capitalist road; there is the danger of capitalist restoration, and there is the danger of subversion and aggression by imperialism and socialist imperialism." It is therefore no wonder that the world will hear about "political instability" in China at periodic intervals. The Chinese take pride in these movements toward the path of "true socialism." They also point out the progress China achieved as a result of the Cultural Revolution.

In the course of providing for leadership after Chou En-lai and Chairman Mao, China seems to have developed a collective decision-making process in which three pillars of the Chinese society—peasants, workers, and army—are well represented. There will, no doubt, be some shifts here and there, but one thing seems clear: China is a nation united and dedicated to upholding the country's basic national security interests. Its people are determined "to build China into a modern and strong socialist state." Mao's teaching inspired the new generation with an urge to continue their "march forward." His educational policy led millions of educated young Chinese to apply themselves to the development of their country. I met many young men and women who are working with an ardent revolutionary spirit. A nation so conscious of its past humiliation and suffering due to colonial exploitation, so fully aware of the dangers from external forces, and so proud of its present achievements and future possibilities, runs no risk of being torn by civil strife after Mao's death. As a Chinese friend told me, "Mao, the individual human being, will die, but Mao, the great teacher, will remain immortal."

Those engaged in working out U.S. policy alternatives toward the Asian Pacific region, and toward China in particular, must consider certain obvious facts.

1. China is the central power in the Asian region; therefore, no important issues in˙ that area can be decided without considering China.

2. The expansionist designs of the Soviet Union in the Third World can only be met by meaningful cooperation between Washington and Peking.

3. China has the potential to become a superpower with tremendous appeal to Afro-Asian countries.

The former U.S. Defense Secretary, James Schlesinger, who was in China when Mao died on December 9, 1976, made the forecast that there would be no "political turmoil; Chairman Mao himself provided a unifying force. The leadership fully recognized that it is now in their common interest to avoid serious political schisms."[129] An earlier visitor, Audrey Topping, the daughter of Canadian diplomat, Mr. Chester Ronning, accompanied her father to China in 1971 and wrote, "There is a power no visitor to modern China can fail to

discern: people power. Nearly eight hundred million people all thinking the same thoughts, reading the same books, talking about the
same things, living in a similar style."[130] My own reaction after my
recent visit to China in July-August 1976 is the same: China shall
continue to march forward. The succession from Chairman Mao to
Chairman Hua seems to have substantiated the confidence expressed
by recent visitors to China. Hua Kuo-feng, who was appointed
Premier, is now Chairman of the Chinese Communist party and
holder of the key positions in the party, in the state, and also in the
army. The four members of the politburo, including Mao's widow,
have been purged and arrested: They are Chiang Ching, Wang Hung-
wen, Chang Chun-chiao, and Yao Wen-yuan.[131] They are known,
according to western press and terminology, as "radicals," as opposed
"moderates" like Chairman Hua, but the Chinese refuse to accept
such distinctions. I have talked extensively with senior Chinese diplomats in Washington and at the UN mission in New York, who inter-
pret the groups in China as two: the "true Marxist-Leninist-Maoist"
group and the few "revisionists" or "capitalist roaders."

Whatever may be the interpretation by China experts all over the
world or by the Chinese themselves, one important fact has emerged
from the succession in China: Chairman Mao's unifying forces have
triumphed. The Chinese people have accepted the decision of the
Communist party without much turmoil or bloodshed, not to speak
of civil war. There are reports of disturbances in some provinces but
none of a real threat to China's stability and continued progress.

It is too early to predict what will be the policies, both internal
and external, of the new leaders in China, but we may say that China
will probably continue to pursue policies best suited to her national,
regional, and global interests.

Will China Continue the Post-Cultural Revolution Foreign Policy of Mao and Chou?

The former Chinese foreign minister, in China's first major foreign
policy statement after Mao's death, told the 31st session of the UN
General Assembly on October 5, 1967, "Strategically, Europe is the
focus of contention between the Soviet Union and the United States
for world hegemony. The so-called 'European Security Conference'
was, in fact, a 'European Insecurity Conference'."[132] "There are
always some people in the West who want to urge social-imperialism

eastward and divert this peril towards China, thinking it best if all is quiet in the West. The 'European Security Conference' reflected such a Munich line of thinking."[133] He continued, "The rivalry between the two superpowers, the Soviet Union and the United States, extends to all parts of the globe. The United States has vested interests to protect around the world, and the Soviet Union seeks expansion. This state of affairs is unalterable. In this world-wide rivalry, the expansionist activities of the Soviet Union are all-pervasive."[134] He also commented: "Following Chairman Mao Tse-tung's teachings, the Chinese government and people firmly and unswervingly support the just struggles of all oppressed nations and oppressed peoples." He concluded by saying, "Chairman Mao Tse-tung taught us that *'In our international relations, we Chinese people should get rid of great-power chauvinism resolutely, thoroughly, wholly, and completely.'* We will follow this instruction of Chairman Mao in handling all our foreign relations."[135]

Chairman Hua in one of his major speeches said, "Both internally and internationally, we shall unswervingly forge ahead along the course charted by Chairman Mao. We are determined to accomplish the sacred cause of liberating Taiwan and reunifying our mother-land."[136] "We are determined to uphold the principles of proletarian internationalism, carry out the revolutionary line and policies in foreign affairs formulated by Chairman Mao, strengthen our unity with the international proletariat and the oppressed nations and op-pressed people of the world, strengthen countries suffering from imperialist and social-imperialist aggression, subversion, intervention, control, and bullying, so as to oppose the hegemonism of the two superpowers—the Soviet Union and the United States."[137]

In our previous chapters, we have pointed out (a) China's quest for security, (b) the early Sino-Soviet friendship transformed into a Sino-Soviet rift, and (c) China's favorable response to President Nixon's friendly gestures in the context of its growing fears of Soviet aggression. A stronger NATO, a stronger ANZUZ, and a stronger Japan have become common objectives of Washington and Peking in the last six or seven years (1970-1976), while, despite so much talk about detente, there seem to be few common objectives between Washington and Moscow.

What will be the fate of "the great power triangle," Washington-Moscow-Peking, in the post-Mao era? Most American authorities feel that the triangular relationship since 1972 has been favorable to the United States and should be maintained: Nixon's opening up relations with China brought a number of diplomatic gains to the United States, including new strength to the U.S. diplomatic dealings with the Soviet Union.

"The problems today in our bilateral relations with both countries are complex," said John Davis. "They are compounded by the fact that each of them at present would like to see our relations with the other deteriorate and is inclined to regard any sign of improved U.S. relations with the other as at least potentially adverse to its own interests."[138] To maintain the present triangular diplomacy, Doak A. Barnett favored "swerving in the direction of full diplomatic relations (with China) relatively soon."[139] However, he is not certain if the new Chinese leaders will continue Mao and Chou's new policy toward the United States. Barnett also feels that "Japan, as an Asian power, feels it very important to have a viable relationship with China."[140] Schlesinger scoffed, "We are not going to swerve at all towards an even-handed policy between Russia and China...."[141] Donald Zagoria believes that "a limited reconciliation between Moscow and Peking is possible after the death of Mao, and that is not in our interest.... I believe the United States should act now to consolidate the Chinese state in a long-term relationship with the United States.... I am advocating the complete normalization of our relations with the People's Republic of China. This is something that should have been done a long time ago."[142]

The Problem of Taiwan in the Sino-American Relationship

The recent debate in the United States over future relations with Taiwan is causing much concern among Chinese officials. They are wondering whether this is a deliberate attempt to postpone the establishment of diplomatic relations between Washington and Peking, or whether it means a reversal of the 1972 communiqué or of the promises made during the 1969-1971 secret negotiations between the two countries.

The Taiwan debate has raised a number of questions. The foremost one is, should the United States unilaterally abrogate a security pact with an ally?[143] In referring to this question, Chinese officials asked me during my 1976 visit to China: "What happened to the U.S. security pacts with Pakistan?" There were four security pacts with Pakistan—two bilateral and two multilateral (SEATO and CENTO). In the 1950s and early 1960s, Pakistan used to be described as "the most allied ally of the United States in Asia." Yet, when India attacked Pakistan by crossing her international boundary on September 6, 1965, the United States did not come to its rescue, though the security pacts required such action as is made clear by the following unqualified statement issued by the U.S. ambassador: "Under instructions from the White House and Department of State (it is acknowledged) positively and without equivocation that our formal agreement to assist Pakistan in the event of aggression, even with our armies, was not limited to communist countries but indeed specifically included India."[144] Then in 1971, under Moscow's direct supervision and guidance, Pakistan was dismembered by Indian troops.

After witnessing such an experience, the Chinese ask, "Why is so much sanctity attached to the security pact with Taiwan?" All countries of the world that have diplomatic ties with China agree with the 1972 communiqué that there are not "two Chinas." Taiwan is not just an island or a piece of territory the Chinese can be expected to forget. It represents to them a rebel or rival government which still pretends to represent the Chinese people and which was unjustly allowed to do so at the United Nations for more than two decades. The Canadian prime minister's decision not to allow the Taiwan team to participate in the 1975 Olympics with the designation of "Republic of China" was greatly appreciated by the Chinese, who consider that the Canadian government's decision accurately reflects Chinese feelings on Taiwan.

I am not, however, suggesting that the United States should do nothing to prevent the use of force in settling the issue. The Chinese indicated more than once that they are prepared to "take long-term views" of it, and Senator Hugh Scott during his visit to China in July 1976 obtained their assurances to this effect again. Since the Sino-American rapprochement came to pass, China has done nothing to cause embarrassment to the United States, and, given a fair opportunity, it should continue to show restraint and do nothing to damage U.S. prestige and the U.S. image in Asia.

The Taiwan debate has given rise to suggestions of a UN-supervised plebiscite in Taiwan. In response to this, the Chinese ask why the United States and other Western powers did not bother to ask for a plebiscite in any of the East European countries before signing the Helsinki document which Solzhenitsyn termed a "moral sellout of those countries and people under Kremlin rule."[145]

Chinese officials are further dismayed by Japan's opposition to the establishment of full diplomatic relations between the United

States and China. They resented the statement by Japanese foreign minister Miyazawa, made during Senator Mike Mansfield's visit to Tokyo in July 1976, that the United States should not break its relationship with Taiwan. Accusing Miyazawa of violating the 1972 China-Japan normalization agreement, which declared that "Taiwan was a part of China," Chiao Kuan-hua said, in reply to his Japanese counterpart, that Japan "has interfered with China's domestic affairs by proposing a two-China policy." Peking has raised no objections to the presence of U.S. troops or bases in Japan; it approves the special relationship between Washington and Tokyo. It is, however, worried about Soviet expansionist designs in Northeast Asia—the prevention of which it feels should be a common objective of both the United States and China.

Taiwan is the most complicating factor in the future Sino-American relationship. There have been suggestions in some quarters that China will take a "long-term" view of the Taiwan issue and that China is more concerned about detente between the United States and the Soviet Union. But let me stress that "liberation of Formosa," or the concept of "one China," is an article of faith with the Chinese leaders. When the secret negotiations between Peking and Washington began in 1969-1971, channeled through Pakistan President Yahya, Chinese leaders, including Mao and Chou En-lai, made it clear in unqualified terms that full normalization of relations with the United States would be "impossible" without settling the issue of Taiwan. In the 1972 Shanghai communiqué, the Chinese made their position on Taiwan very clear. My Chinese friends in Peking, as well as in London, Cairo, Washington, and New York, told me on numerous occasions that they had made their views on Taiwan clear to all American visitors, including Presidents Nixon and Ford, Henry Kissinger, senators, and other high-ranking American dignitaries. When questioned about their "long-term" solution of Formosa, their answer has constantly been: "We are reasonable and patient. We do not want to put pressure on any country, including the United States, but our patience and friendly attitude should not make any country take our friendship for granted or consider our patience unlimited."

The Chinese have laid down three conditions for the full normalization of relations with the United States:

1. the recall of the U.S. ambassador from Taiwan and subsequent installment of an ambassador in Peking,

2. the abrogation of the United States-Formosa Security Pact of 1954, and

3. the withdrawal of the U.S. armed forces from Taiwan.

The Chinese cannot also afford to give a public promise not to use force to settle the Formosa issue. They consider Formosa an "integral part" and "internal problem" of China. Like any other great power, China feels that no other country can be allowed to dictate how it should resolve its own "internal problem."

After careful analysis of my talks with Chinese leaders and diplomats and also after assessing China's attitude toward Formosa from some other reliable diplomatic sources—diplomats of those countries with which China has close, friendly ties—I shall make the following assessment of the above-mentioned demands by China for the solution of the Formosa issue.

1. The U.S. ambassador from Taiwan should be withdrawn and full diplomatic relations at ambassadorial levels should be established between Peking and Washington without any further delay, if the Sino-American relationship is expected to have any meaning in the post-Mao era.

2. The 1954 security pact, which may be described as outdated and obsolete, should be given a quiet burial. The Chinese cannot expect the United States to formally and publicly abrogate the 1954 security pact, but many treaties die without formal abrogation. For example, the 1950 Sino-Soviet alliance is not yet formally abrogated, though the two countries now consider each other enemies. The United States has allowed to lapse security treaties with some of its Asian allies, such as the security treaty with Pakistan of 1954 (secretly renewed in 1964) and the bilateral treaty of 1959. Similarly the United States cannot expect a formal and public declaration from Peking "not to use force" in settlement of the Formosa issue. But no government in China will resort, I strongly believe, to force if they wish to retain the goodwill and friendship of the United States. The Chinese realize fully the strong sentiment in favor of Taiwan among the U.S. policy makers. The Chinese aims are to continue and develop friendship with the United States and not to destroy the friendship by a unilateral resort to force in Taiwan which will have adverse repercussions in the United States.

The United States is now in a dilemma, caught between the 1954 security pact and the 1972 communiqué as well as informal secret pledges made in 1969-1971. Senator Mike Mansfield, after his visit to China on September 27-October 12, 1976, after the death of Mao, correctly summed up the situation with regard to the U.S. security pact with Formosa:

There can hardly be a continuance of a defense treaty with one faction in a civil war while formal relations are maintained with the successor. When Japan recognized the People's Republic of China in 1972, its treaty of friendship with Taiwan automatically lapsed. So will the U.S.-Taiwan security treaty. It has been urged that the treaty issue be handled by serving one-year notice of our intention to terminate the treaty, a right reserved to each under article X. This course would only further confuse the principle at issue. If Taiwan is part of China, as the concerned parties now agree, serving a one-year notice to terminate the treaty means only additional delay in reconciling our official diplomatic posture and our national policy. . . .They are national commitments subject to adjustment in the light of changing international realities and clearer perception of the national interest. The treaty was based in great part on U.S. security needs against Moscow-directed axis with Peking, which is now seen to be a distortion. Moreover, the government of Taiwan claims to represent the people on the mainland, but it does not. It has ruled the island of Taiwan by martial law since 1949 in order to continue the trappings of a government for the entire Chinese mainland. Only 86 of the 1,288 seats in the National Assembly of the Republic of China and 49 of the 436 seats in the Legislative Yuan are held by the Taiwanese.[146]

Senator Mansfield's view is shared by Senator Hugh Scott who visited China July 10-24, 1976. He wrote in his report,

From what the Chinese said to me about Taiwan, I draw several inferences. Last December, Peking was prepared to understand and to acquiesce in some delay in the U.S. actions necessary to establish full diplomatic relations with the People's Republic of China. China, however, is not willing to acquiesce in such postponement for an indefinite period of time, and they used such terms as "unrealistic and unacceptable." Whereas Peking, for some time, has been talking with us about a variety of mutual concerns in the global arena, with lessened emphasis on China's concern over the unresolved Taiwan issue, China had done this because it believed that its unchanging interest in resolution of this part of China's unfinished civil war had been taken for granted by us.

My second inference arises from the state of mind caused by the death of Premier Chou En-lai, the now publicly admitted frailty of Chairman Mao, and what was, to me, an obvious general uncertainty about the composition and likely intentions of China's future leadership. At such time, there was clearly an advantage in moving toward the conclusion of important unfinished business which China had undertaken with the full authority of both Chairman Mao and Premier Chou En-lai: implementation of the Shanghai communique.[147]

The former Senate majority and minority leaders' views on China are also shared by leading American Sinologists, such as Doak Barnett, Donald Zagoria, Paton Davis, and many others. There are, of course, dissenting voices who seem to be unduly concerned about Taiwan's "loyalty" to the United States and about "sanctity" of the 1954 security pact. There are also powerful Taiwanese lobbyists in Washington who, as pointed out earlier, intensified their activities in the 1976 U.S. election year and are now engaged in influencing the new Carter administration.

There will be no threat to U.S. economic ties and trade with Formosa from full U.S. diplomatic relations with China. The Chinese are willing to accept the "Japan Formula" under which Japan, while having full diplomatic relations with Peking, is also continuing its economic relations with Formosa. China is prepared to accept the "Japan Formula" in her relations with the United States but not the "German Formula," under which the United States has diplomatic relations with the two "Germanies."

3. The final basic requirement of China for a solution to the Formosa issue would be the withdrawal of U.S. troops from Taiwan. The process of the withdrawal of U.S. troops has already begun. U.S. military personnel in Taiwan were reduced to 2,300 by mid-1976. The U.S. troops have also left the off-shore islands, Quemoy and Matsu. The United States quietly withdrew its last combat aircraft based in Taiwan.[148]

But the reports of the United States carrying out an increased arms sales program to Taiwan caused irritation to Peking. There was also an upsetting report that a Taiwanese team of engineers are working at the Massachusetts Institute of Technology "to develop a medium-range missile and a nuclear device."[149] If Taiwan develops any atomic weapons, the result could be an attack of Formosa by China, which, as I am told repeatedly by the Chinese, will not allow Taiwan to have such weapons.

What are the strategic values of Taiwan to the United States? What are the *quid pro quos* for Chinese friendship at the cost of "an ally"? Idealism and morality should not be abandoned totally in international politics, nor should politics be determined only in terms of "goodwill," "loyalty," etc. The friends of Taiwan often refer to the unqualified "loyalty" of Taiwan to the United States. But what else, one may ask, could Taiwan do except look toward Washington? Taiwan is the foster child of the United States, a product of the cold war during the Eisenhower-Dulles era. In the 1970s, Taiwan has no substantial strategic importance or value to the United States. But, as I have already said, that does not imply that Taiwan should be abandoned to the mercy of "Communist China," which they regard as an enemy—but who are "they"? They are a small and corrupt ruling elite; eighty-five percent of the original Taiwanese people have hardly any role in the present regime of Taiwan. I feel—again from my talks with Chinese friends—that the best guarantee for Taiwan's ultimate survival is a good and lasting Sino-American relationship. The remaining U.S. troops cannot protect Taiwan, unless the United States is ready ro resort to nuclear war against China. And China has made the possibly correct assessment that the

United States would not like to see China destroyed by a nuclear war—if not out of love for the Chinese, then from concern to maintain the current balance of power between Washington, Moscow, and Peking. The destruction of China would be a boon to the Kremlin which the United States cannot afford to grant. Nor is China sure if the United States can afford another Vietnam-type war in Taiwan. (Let me note, however, that the Chinese are prepared to see the continued presence of the U.S. Seventh Fleet in the Pacific and are opposed to the total withdrawal of U.S. troops from the Asian-Pacific region.)

If China becomes convinced that the Formosa issue will not be settled by the development of the Sino-American relationship, they may, I am really inclined to believe, resort to force to "liberate" Taiwan, which will have terrible consequences not only for the Sino-American relationship but also for other Asian countries, including Japan. In his memorial speech at Mao's funeral, Chairman Hua said, "We are determined to accomplish the sacred cause of liberating Taiwan and reunifying our Motherland."[150] After being elected chairman of the Chinese Communist party, Hua reaffirmed his pledge with regard to Taiwan on December 25.[151] The Chinese Scientific Association made a strongly-worded pledge regarding Taiwan: "There is only one China in the World, that is, the People's Republic of China. Taiwan is one of the provinces and an inalienable part of the People's Republic of China." The statement was made in response to a resolution of the 16th General Assembly of the International Council of Scientific Unions held in Washington in November 1976 suggesting the concept of "Two Chinas." [152]

Before I conclude my discussion on Formosa, let me also reaffirm that in recent months there are growing signs of impatience on the part of China over what they term "undue" delay in normalization of relations between the United States and China. There are also frequent hints about "ultimately resorting to force" if the United States takes China's patience or friendship for granted. The sooner this complex issue in the Sino-American relations is resolved by negotiations, the better for world peace and for the mutual interests of both China and the United States.

The Sino-Soviet Relationship in the Post-Mao Era

At the moment, chances of a Sino-Soviet rapprochement are very limited. On the eve of Mao's death, China's former foreign minister Chiao Kua-hua, in a September 8, 1976 welcoming speech to former U.S. Defense Secretary James Schlesinger, said,

> The imperialist power that styles itself socialist used the rhetoric of 'detente' most vociferously while most energetically expanding its armaments and preparing for war. As Dr. Schlesinger has rightly pointed out, it 'talks peace, but it practices war.' Confronted with the expansionist ambitions of this superpower, some people try appeasement and concession or even sacrifice others in an attempt to protect themselves. This is, of course, wishful thinking. The lesson of Munich in the thirties proves that to do so can only mean rearing a tiger cub and bringing ultimate disaster upon oneself. In our opinion, the correct policy should be to face reality, mobilize and rely on the people, and unite with all the forces that can be united with to wage a tit-for-tat struggle against it.[153]

The former Chinese foreign minister told the 1976 UN General Assembly, "The Soviet Union is trying to expand its influence in the world, and it ultimately will wind up in a war with the United States." In addition to the usual Chinese denunciation of Soviet "social imperialism" and "expansionist activities," Chiao declared that Europeans and developing countries should shake off any fear of the Kremlin, because its outward appearance of strength was undermined by internal dissension. "There is now a strange phenomenon in the world," Chiao said. "Some people are terrified at the mention of the Soviet Union, thinking that it cannot be touched. This is superstition. Soviet social imperialism is nothing to be afraid of. It is outwardly strong but inwardly weak."[154]

The vital issue is whether the United States and her allies should assume the Sino-Soviet rift—and Chinese friendship—to be permanent. To do so, I feel, would be a fatal mistake. In international politics, there are no eternal friends or eternal enemies; there are only eternal interests. It is true that the Sino-Soviet relationship may be affected by many factors other than the U.S. policy towards Peking or Moscow, but at the present phase of the triangular Moscow-Peking-Washington relationship, U.S. policy is of vital importance. The United States cannot ensure a continuation of the Sino-Soviet rift in the post-Mao period but, by avoiding a "cooling off" in the Sino-American relationship, can certainly reduce the chances of a Sino-Soviet rapprochement. Undue concern over "abandoning an ally" (Taiwan) may ultimately create some bigger problems for the United States than would be created by the actual "abandoning."

I should point out one danger in the undue delay in normalization of Sino-American relations: The Chinese may come to believe, rightly or wrongly, that the United States is utilizing its "China connection" as leverage in its bargaining position with Moscow. I have strong feelings that, within the Chinese leadership, a group which, from the beginning has not been happy with China's "flirting" with America, might start arguing as follows: "We have tried the Americans; why don't we try the Russians now? Neither of them are our friends. But we have waited five years for the Americans; why not pause a while and look to Moscow for a better deal." This argument is more likely to be voiced now that Mao and Chou En-lai are dead.

The Chinese friendship is worthy of American trust. China has no hegemonic aspirations in the Asian-Pacific area. Recalling the proverb, "A stitch in time saves nine," the United States should avail itself of China's good will and friendship before China's patience is taxed too far. That would be a tragic end to the great U.S. diplomatic feat begun in 1970-1972.

The "Soviet Factor" in China's Triangular Diplomacy

Apart from the Formosa issue, the "Soviet factor," or the Soviet-American detente, is another important and complicating factor in the future Sino-American relationship. There is no doubt that China is keenly watching the U.S.-USSR detente for the future pattern of relations between superpowers, including the problems and prospects of a SALT II agreement. Like any other country, China will try to achieve a favorable balance of world power from the standpoint of its own security and basic national interests. As pointed out by George Modelski, foreign policy is the system of activities evolved by communities for changing the behavior of other states and for adjusting their own activities to the international environment. The fact that the behavior of one state affects other states confronts every state with the problem, to quote Modelski again, of minimizing adverse actions and maximizing favorable actions of foreign states. Thus, foreign policy is essentially a question of states adjusting to each other.[155] China is no exception to this fundamental rule of the game of international politics.

As pointed out earlier, China would not concede that her attitude to the United States is dependent on the Soviet-American relations. The·Chinese also seem convinced that there can be no genuine friendship or detente between Moscow and Washington. They dismiss the idea of any genuine arms agreement between Moscow and Washington. Yet when SALT I was signed in Moscow on May 26, 1972, China's initial reaction was one of silence for two months. Then, in July 1972, Premier Chou En-lai delivered the Chinese reaction. He termed the SALT I agreement a "new weapons race between the United States and the Soviet Union" and stated, "In order to contend for world hegemony, they (the United States and the Soviet Union) are engaged in an arms race not only in nuclear armaments but also in conventional armaments, each trying to gain superiority. . . . One of the main objectives of the fraudulent U.S. imperialist-Soviet revisionist agreements on disarmament remains that of hindering the consolidation of the defense capacity of the People's Republic of China."[156]

The Chinese continue to be skeptical about the Moscow-Washington arms agreement, preferring to recall former Secretary of Defense Laird's and also Schlesinger's warnings about the huge Soviet military build-up in spite of negotiations for SALT II.[157] The Chinese are not happy over President Carter's giving top priority to SALT II, his willingness to meet Brezhnev in 1977, possibly in the United States, and his not mentioning anything about "normalization of relations" with China.

One may ask, why should the Americans worry about the Chinese reaction to the Soviet-American relationship? However, in the present triangular relationship of the great powers, China is as much entitled to express concerns over the detente between Moscow and Washington as the Americans are to express interest, if not worry, over any prospect of a Sino-Soviet thaw, or what is termed "Bear-Dragon flirtation."[158] The Americans realize that, in the absence of Chinese hostility, the Soviet Union would become for Washington an uncontrollable "bear" in many parts of the world, including Japan, the NATO countries, the Middle East, and Africa. Similarly, the Chinese realize that if the two superpowers reach a genuine understanding, the Soviet's menacing threats to China will be extremely serious. So it is in the interest of China to prevent any meaningful understanding between Moscow and Washington, just as Moscow considers it constructive diplomacy if they can frustrate the emerging Sino-American relationship.

Contrary to many speculations, the transition from Chairman Mao to Chairman Hua has been peaceful. The ousting of four leaders should not be regarded as anything special because purging in a communist system is a normal practice. The fact that, in China, purging involving Mao's widow has not caused any street fighting or upheaval proves that here is a nation united and dedicated to uphold its own interests.

China in the post-Mao era will not be the same as it was under Mao, just as India under Nehru's daughter was not the same as it was under Nehru. But India is still pursuing its national interests in the same way; India is militarily even stronger. So the determination of the exact nature of Chinese communism in the post-Mao era is a matter which, I believe, we may leave to the Chinese to work out for themselves.

Will Mao's successors respond to Moscow's bids for a thaw? The Kremlin leaders have shown interest in reducing tensions in the Sino-Soviet rift. From reliable sources (other than Chinese), I have come to know that Russia has sent "feelers" to Peking, directly as well as indirectly, i.e., through third countries. The chief editor of the *Pravda* claimed that there were good prospects of better relations with Peking.[159] Peking has not yet "officially" responded. The Chinese diplomat did not walk out of the Kremlin reception on the anniversary of the Russian Revolution, November 7, nor did the Russian Defense Minister make any adverse comment on China. (China also sent a nice note to the Soviet Union for the occasion.) But, within three days, the Chinese revived their routine attack on the Russians, calling Brezhnev a "liar," and the Soviet ambassador walked out of a reception in Peking.[160]

What do all these incidents indicate? I personally feel that the Chinese are now in a period of "reappraisal" and "rethinking" in their foreign policy objectives. It appears to me that they want some beginning of "normalization of relations" with the United States. They will not—and this is my honest assessment—wait indefinitely. They will give the Carter administration sufficient time, but, if no move in the direction of normalization takes place, they may give a "smile" towards Moscow which has already shown interest in such "smiles." It is for the Americans to decide which is more important: Taiwan or a thaw in the Sino-Soviet relationship which will upset the present balance of power between Washington, Moscow, and Peking. Chairman Hua cannot overnight say that "the Soviet Union is now our good neighbor," but, in a highly controlled and indoctrinated society like China or the Soviet Union, it is not difficult either to make changes from one extreme political stance to another.

Neither China nor the Soviet Union is a friend of the United States. Therefore, the United States should create a situation where the chance of a Sino-Soviet thaw is as small as possible. Its "love" and "concern" for an outdated treaty with Taiwan should not make the United States neglect its vital security and global interests.

The Chinese are anxiously waiting to see the Carter administration's China policy. I think that they will not respond to Soviet gestures until they know the policy of the new U.S. administration. They are very anxious to retain U.S. friendship, but, as I could gather from my conversations, the new Chinese leaders would not be able to satisfy the army and the people unless the United States takes some steps to normalize the Sino-American relationship. They may take various forms, but *some steps,* I feel, are urgently required to prevent Peking from falling into the trap of the Soviet's game.

President Carter and China

The Chinese have indicated concern about President Carter's active pursuit of military detente with Moscow. They have been keenly watching for any sign of progress toward a SALT II agreement, feeling unhappy, as pointed out earlier, that improved U.S. relations with China seem to have less priority on President Carter's "priority list" of foreign policy goals than does this agreement with Moscow. Therefore, the failure of Secretary of State Vance's arms talks with the Russians in Moscow, from March 26-30, 1977, gave the Chinese real pleasure. The *Peking Review* gleefully wrote,

> Talks between U.S. Secretary of State Cyrus Vance and the Soviet leaders on the major question of the "strategic arms limitation" from March 26-30 ended without any progress.
> In the Moscow talks, Vance presented the Soviet side with two alternative proposals.
> The Soviet Union rejected both proposals. It called for a formal agreement on the Vladivostok accord and insisted that the U.S. Cruise missile should be included in the count while the Soviet Backfire bomber be left out. The Soviet demand was turned down by the U.S. side.
> Nuclear weapons are the lifeline of the Soviet Union and the United States in their rivalry for world hegemony. Each tries to limit the other through talks so as to expand itself. That is why the SALT talks, which have been conducted for several years, have come to naught and the nuclear arms of both countries have been developing unchecked. The recent Moscow talks were nothing more than haggling in the struggle between Moscow and Washington.[161]

After the failure of Vance's mission to Moscow, the United States began to take a fresh look at the Sino-American relationship.

However, President Carter, in his address to the United Nations on March 27, 1977, had already said, "We will continue our efforts to develop further our relationship with the People's Republic of China. We recognize our parallel strategic interests in maintaining stability in Asia and will act in the spirit of the Shanghai communiqué."[162] The Chinese seemed to be pleased by President Carter's reference to the Shanghai communiqué and lack of reference to the Taiwan issue.

When China's UN ambassador, Huang Chen, met with President Carter in February 1977, he reminded Carter of U.S. promises and assurances about full diplomatic relations between the United States and China. Secretary of State Vance was reported to have checked into whether Nixon or Kissinger had made any informal commitment to Peking about full diplomatic relations,[163] and it was finally disclosed that President Nixon had made such a promise during his first China visit: Nixon had indicated that full diplomatic relations with China would be established after his reelection in 1973.[164]

After the unsuccessful Vance mission to Msocow over the SALT II agreement, there are "increasing signs" that the Carter administration is giving "more attention" to China. The president's son, Chip Carter, accompanied a congressional delegation to China in April 1977. The administration has been talking of the need "to normalize relations with Peking before the end of the year."[165] Secretary Vance has a tentative plan to visit China in November 1977, and by then Carter's "China policy" is expected to be finalized.

Talks have also started, without any publicity, to settle financial claims between the United States and China. Financial claims go back to 1950. On December 19, 1950, the United States blocked dollar bank accounts and other Chinese assets in the United States amounting to about $80 million because of China's intervention in the Korean war. China also blocked $200 million worth of American assets in China. Financial claims have not been as important as Taiwan or the detente between the United States and the Soviet Union, but still they have been a vexing, complicating factor in the Sino-American relationship. Kissinger made attempts to resolve the issue but with no success. When Ambassador Huang Chen met President Carter in February 1977, the issue was raised.

Although the U.S. officials will not acknowledge that they view relations with China as a way of bringing pressure on the Russians, this has always been implicit in the great power triangle between Washington, Moscow, and Peking. Joseph Kraft wrote, "Peking remains a major diplomatic asset to the United States. . . . China and the ideological and real threats it poses to Russia's claim to lead the communist world is still one of the best things Washington has going against Moscow."[166]

Donald Zagoria lists the benefits derived by the United States from the Sino-Soviet dispute. Militarily, he says, half of the Soviet armed forces are tied down on the Chinese border, which gives Moscow a strong incentive to avoid a crisis in the West. Ideologically, Peking is challenging Moscow in the Third World and in the international Communist movement. Politically, Moscow must contend with the virulent, worldwide campaign against Soviet influence. Diplomatically, the dispute has given Washington diplomatic leverage against Moscow—something that Brzezinski himself has stressed on a number of occasions.[167]

Zagoria's recommendation is that, to preserve these advantages, Washington should "tilt" towards Peking by accelerating the process of normalization with China. He believes that a formula could be found which would preserve the independence of Taiwan without compromising Peking's claim to sovereignty over the island. He says that while U.S. arms should not be sold "directly" to China, Washington should facilitate such sales by allies.[168]

Initial Chinese reaction to the failure of the Vance talks in Moscow and the Carter administration's "playing the Chinese card" was, no doubt, favorable. I had lengthy talks with Chinese diplomats in Washington and New York in April and May 1977; they made reserved comments, yet I could gather that they were pleased with the latest developments in the Washington-Moscow-Peking relationship. But then came rather strongly worded comments from the Chinese Ministry of Foreign Affairs in Peking. A senior Chinese official has expressed great dissatisfaction with the Carter administration's failure so far to move toward full diplomatic relations with Peking. "We have not found any sign. . .of a decision being taken by the United States to resolve the problem," the official said in an interview. "In other words, there is no sign in sight at this point that the United States has made up its mind to discuss normalizing relations between our two countries."[169]

These remarks were apparently the first strong criticism by Peking of the Carter administration's China policy. The Chinese official, who asked not to be identified, said that Carter and Vance "are talking about how they will not discount their old friends, and of course they are talking about a small handful of people like Chiang Chingkuo." (Chiang is premier of the Nationalist Chinese government in Taiwan, whose continued relations with Washington are the main obstacle to normalization.) American talk about sticking with Taiwan "runs counter to the spirit of the Shanghai communiqué," the official said. "The responsibility for the lack of development in Sino-American relations doesn't rest on the Chinese side, it rests completely on the Americans'."[170]

To my queries about these remarks, the Chinese diplomats in the United States would not comment. They said only, "We believe in principles and not in expediencies. We could have taken advantage of the United States by exploiting the bogey of a Sino-Soviet rapprochement, about which our American friends are worried; but we do not believe in such tactics." They are of the opinion that the U.S. government should fulfill the commitments made in 1969-1971 and also at the time of the Shanghai communiqué.

From my talks in April and May of 1977 with the senior Chinese diplomats in Washington and New York, I am inclined to believe that the Chinese will not make any compromise on the issue of "one China"—i.e., Taiwan must be regarded as part of China. This does not, however, mean that the Chinese would resort to arms as soon as the U.S. ambassador is moved from Taiwan to Peking. On the contrary, the normalization of the Sino-American relationship with full diplomatic relations will offer the best guarantee for Taiwan and for peace and stability in the Asia-Pacific region. More important, the Soviet expansionist designs in the Third World will be deterred by a meaningful Sino-American relationship.

President Carter was asked during his news conference on May 13, 1977 if he had a "target date" for full diplomatic recognition of the P.R.C. "within his first administration." Carter's reply was:

> It's very difficult for me to set a target date because this is a two-way negotiation. We have commenced discussions with the Chinese government to resolve the first obstacle, and that is a claims settlement. Long years ago, we had roughly $190 million worth of American property and other goods confiscated by the Mao Tse-tung government. We in our country confiscated in return about $80 million, I believe, primarily in Chinese bank deposits. We've never been able to work out those differing claims. That would be the first step.
>
> We have espoused, and I have renewed my commitment, to the Shanghai Conference, the Shanghai Communiqué, which says that there's just one China—we didn't say which one, and neither did anyone else—and we have moved, I think, to strengthen our ties with the People's Republic of China. I have met personally with Ambassador Huang. Cy Vance has met several times with him. We've sent a delegation of congressmen over there, along with my own son, as a demonstration, a gesture of friendship. They were well received.
>
> The one obstacle—major obstacle—obviously is the relationship we've always had with Taiwan. We don't want to see the Taiwanese people punished or attacked.

And if we can resolve that major difficulty I would move expeditiously to normalizing relationships with China. But I can't put a time limit on it.[171]

A senior Chinese diplomat told me on May 6, 1977 that in the fifth volume of "Selected Works of Mao Tse-tung," which has just been published in Chinese (not yet translated into English), Mao expressed the view that it might take 100 years to have "full diplomatic relations with the U.S.A." Richard Nixon, in his second television interview with David Frost on May 13, 1977, narrated how Mao told Kosygin "our differences are going to continue ten thousand years"; then Kosygin said, "Mr. Chairman, after these long discussions we have, don't you think that you could reduce that number somewhat?" Mao's reply was, "Well, in view of the very persuasive arguments that the Premier (Kosygin) has made, I will knock off a thousand years. Our disputes will continue for nine thousand years."[172]

If the Chinese take such "long term" views, the U.S.-China full diplomatic relationship may still have a long period of waiting. Let us hope that it's not a correct assessment of the situation.

Footnotes

1. Marcus Conlife, ed., *The Times History of Our Times* (London: Weidenfeld and Nicolson, 1971), pp. 285-286.

2. Mike Mansfield, *China Enters the Post-Mao Era: A Report by Senator Mike Mansfield, Majority Leader, U.S. Senate,* Report No. 3, Committee on Foreign Relations, United States Senate, November 1976 (Washington, D.C.: U.S. Government Printing Office, 1976).

3. Based on my reading of the Pakistan government's unpublished documents and papers.

4. Ibid., and interviews with Ayub.

5. Ibid.

6. Harold C. Hinton, *An Introduction to Chinese Politics* (New York: Praeger Publishers, 1975), p. 25.

7. See the text of Mao's speech at an enlarged meeting of the political bureau of the Communist party of China (CCP) Central Committee, on April 25, 1956, *New China News Analysis* (Peking), December 25, 1975.

8. See Fox Butterfield, "Mao Tse-tung: Father of the Chinese Revolution," *New York Times,* September 10, 1975.

9. See *United States-Soviet Union-China: The Great Power Triangle,* hearings before the Subcommittee on Future Foreign Policy Research and Development of the Committee on International Relations, House of Representatives, 96th Congress (Washington, D.C.: U.S. Government Printing Office, 1976), part 1, p. 10.

10. Ibid, pp. 62-63.

11. Ibid.

12. *China and the U.S. Far East Policy, 1965-1966,* a publication of the Congressional Quarterly Service, 1735 K Street, N.W., Washington, D.C. 20006, p. 47.

13. Ibid, p. 48.

14. *Selected Works of Mao Tse-tung* (Peking: Foreign Language Press, 1967), vol. 2, p. 335.

15. Ibid.,vol. 3, p. 256.

16. Ibid., vol. 4, p. 415.

17. Ibid., vol. 4, p. 417.

18. *New York Times,* February 16, 1950.

19. *The Sino-Soviet Dispute,* Kessing Research Report No. 3 (New York: Charles Scribner's Sons, 1969), p. 3.

20. G. W. Choudhury, *India, Pakistan, Bangladesh, and the Major Powers: Politics of a Divided Subcontinent* (New York: The Free Press, 1975), p. 147.

21. See Prime Minister Nehru's speech on September 30, 1954 delivered to the Lok Sabha, in *Nehru's Speeches* (New Delhi: Ministry of Information and Broadcasting, Government of India, n.d.)., vol. 3 (1953-1955).

22. Based on my reading of the Pakistan government's unpublished documents and papers and on my interviews with Ayub.

23. Ibid.

24. *United States-Soviet Union-China: The Great Power Triangle,* part 1, p. 10.

25. *New York Times,* February 3, 1953.

26. Foster R. Dulles, *American Policy Toward Communist China, 1949-1969* (New York: Thomas Y. Crowell Company, 1972), p. 132.

27. Ibid., p. 133.

28. Ibid., p. 134.

29. Ibid.

30. John F. Fairbank, *China Perceived: Images and Policies in China-American Relations* (New York: Alfred A. Knopf, 1976), pp. 29-30.

31. *United States-Soviet Union-China: The Great Power Triangle,* part 1, p. 3.

32. Conlife, *The Times History of Our Times,* p. 259.

33. *Pravda* (Moscow), September 10, 1959.

34. *Sino-Soviet Conflict,* A Report on the Sino-Soviet Conflict and its Implications, by the Subcommittee on the Far East and the Pacific of the Committee on Foreign Affairs, U.S. House of Representatives, May 14, 1965 (Washington, D.C.: U.S. Government Printing Office, 1965), p. 112.

35. Ibid., p. 246.

36. Ibid, p. 218.

37. Ibid., pp. 219-220.

38. William E. Griffin, *Peking, Moscow and Beyond,* Washington Paper No. 6 (Washington, D.C.: Center for Strategic and International Studies, Georgetown University, 1973), pp. 10-17.

39. *Statesman* (New Delhi), November 28, 1959.

40. Based on my reading of the Pakistan government's unpublished documents and on interviews with Ayub.

41. Ibid.

42. For details of the agreement, see (a) Harold C. Hinton, *Peking-Washington: Chinese Foreign Policy and the United States,* Washington Paper No. 34 (Washington, D.C.: Center for Strategic and International Studies, Georgetown University, 1976), and (b) *The Sino-Soviet Dispute.*

43. "President Nixon's China Initiative: A Conference Report," *ORBIS,* Winter 1972, p. 1211.

44. For details see *The Sino-Soviet Dispute.*

45. Ibid.

46. Based on my reading of the Pakistan government's unpublished documents and papers.

47. Ibid.

48. Ibid.

49. For details see G. W. Choudhury, *Brezhnev's Collective Security Plan for Asia* (Washington, D.C.: Center for Strategic and International Studies, Georgetown University, 1976).

50. Ibid, p. 16.

51. *Pravda* (Moscow), June 8, 1969.

52. Ibid., September 21, 1969.

53. G. W. Choudhury, *Brezhnev's Collective Security Plan for Asia*, p. 18.

54. *Times of India* (New Delhi), September 18, 1970.

55. Based on my reading of the Pakistan government's unpublished documents and papers.

56. Ibid.

57. Ibid.

58. Ibid.

59. G. W. Choudhury, *Brezhnev's Collective Security Plan for Asia*, p. 40.

60. Based on my reading of the Pakistan government's unpublished documents and on interviews with President Yahya.

61. "The United States, the Soviet Union, and the People's Republic of China," Department of State news release, March 23, 1976.

62. *New York Times*, December 8, 1975.

63. *New York Times*, September 26, 1976.

64. "The United States, the Soviet Union, and the People's Republic of China."

65. C. L. Sulzberger, "Brezhnev's Cruise to China," *New York Times*, July 5, 1975.

66. *Peking Review*, January 30, 1974.

67. *Newsweek*, February 9, 1976.

68. *New York Times*, September 26, 1976.

69. Based on my talks in China during my visit there in July-August 1971, as well as on information gathered through diplomatic sources of friendly countries.

70. *New York Times*, September 12, 1975.

71. See Stephen Barber, "Foreign Relations: Peking A Matter of Time," *Far Eastern Economic Review*, July 2, 1976.

72. Ibid.

73. Based on my reading of the Pakistan government's unpublished documents and papers.

74. David Bonana, "The Wizard That Was," *Far Eastern Economic Review*, July 2, 1976.

75. Stephen Barber, "New Balance of Power," *Far Eastern Economic Review*, July 2, 1976.

76. See Michael J. Deane, "The Soviet Assessment of the Correlation of World Forces: Implications for American Foreign Policy," *ORBIS*, Fall 1976.

77. *Durham* (N.C.) *Morning Herald*, May 22, 1975.

78. *Peking Review*, February 1976.

79. Ibid.

80. *New York Times*, June 4, 1975.

81. Ibid.

82. *Times* (London), May 16, 1976.

83. Jonathan D. Pollack, "Peking's Nuclear Restraints," *New York Times*, April 12, 1976.

101

84. *New York Times,* July 6, 1976.

85. Ibid., September 10, 1962.

86. See Susmi Awanohoro, "Japan Changes Directions," *Far Eastern Economic Review,* October 1, 1976.

87. Joseph Kraft, "Japan's Crucial Role in Sino-American Relations," *Washington Post,* December 17, 1975.

88. Awanohoro, "Japan Changes Directions."

89. Ibid.

90. "Gromyko's Tokyo Rebuff," editorial, *New York Times,* January 19, 1976.

91. *A Study of Japan's Defense Issues,* report of a committee appointed by Defense Minister of State, Michita Sakata (Tokyo: Ministry of Defense, Government of Japan, September 1975), p. 16.

92. Ibid.

93. *Peking Review,* July 30, 1976.

94. Ibid.

95. John Gittings, "Recognition on China's Doorsteps," *The Guardian* (London), May 29, 1974.

96. *Times* (London), February 25, 1976.

97. Based on my talks with Chinese leaders and diplomats in July-August 1976.

98. Based on my reading of the minutes of the talks between Yahya and Chou En-lai in November 1970.

99. For details, see G. W. Choudhury, *India, Pakistan, Bangladesh, and the Major Powers.*

100. *Times of India* (New Delhi), April 16, 1975.

101. See *Far Eastern Economic Review,* October 1, 1976.

102. Based on my reading of the Pakistan government's unpublished documents and papers.

103. Ibid.

104. *Dawn* (Karachi), May 14, 1955.

105. Ibid., November 3, 1965.

106. *Times* (London), June 12, 1971.

107. Based on my research at the Royal Institute of International Affairs in London and the Research Institute on Communist Affairs at Columbia University in New York, 1971-1974.

108. Ibid.

109. Ibid.

110. Ibid.

111. *New York Times,* March 18, 1976.

112. Ibid.

113. See Premier (now Chairman) Hua Kua-feng's speech in honor of President Khama of Botswana, *Peking Review,* July 30, 1976.

114. The Chinese Peoples' Institute of Foreign Affairs, comps., *China Supports the Arab Peoples' Struggle for National Independence: A Selection of Important Documents* (Peking: Foreign Language Press, 1958), p. 1.

115. Ibid., p. 21 (Mao Tse-tung's opening speech at the Eighth National Congress of the Chinese Communist party, September 15, 1956).

116. Ibid., p. 27 (Liu Shao-chi's speech at the Eighth Congress of the Chinese Communist party, September 15, 1956).

117. Speech by Chiao Kua-hua, Chairman of the delegation of the People's Republic of China to the plenary meeting of the thirty-first session of the UN General Assembly (press release by the People's Republic of China Mission to the United Nations, New York, 1976).

118. *New York Times,* April 21 and 22, 1976.

119. See Chiao Kua-hua's speech at the twenty-seventh session of the UN General Assembly (press release by the People's Republic of China Mission to the United Nations, New York, 1972).

120. See Chiao Kua-hua's speech at the twenty-eighth session of the UN General Assembly (press release by the People's Republic of China Mission to the United Nations, New York, 1973).

121. See Chiao Kua-hua's speech at the twenty-ninth session of the UN General Assembly (press release by the People's Republic of China Mission to the United Nations, New York, 1974).

122. Safi Haeri, "Friends for 3,000 Years," *Far Eastern Economic Review,* October 1, 1976.

123. *Times* (London), May 13, 1975.

124. *New China News Agency,* May 12, 1975.

125. *Times* (London), May 18, 1975.

126. See Chairman Hua's speech at the second National Conference on Learning from Taching in Agriculture, *People's Daily* (Peking), December 26, 1976.

127. Ibid.

128. *Peking Review,* January 2, 1973.

129. James Schlesinger, "Inside China Now," *U.S. News and World Report,* October 18, 1976.

130. Audrey Topping, "Return to Changing China," *National Geographic,* December 1971.

131. See *Far Eastern Economic Review,* October 22, 1976.

132. See Chiao Kau-hua's speech at the thirty-first session of the UN General Assembly (press release by the People's Republic of China Mission to the United Nations, October 5, 1976).

133. Ibid., p. 4.

134. Ibid, p. 5.

135. Ibid, p. 8.

136. See Chairman Hua's speech on December 25, 1975.

137. Ibid.

138. *United States-Soviet Union-China: The Great Power Triangle,* part 1, p. 7.

139. Ibid., p. 14.

140. Ibid., p. 26.

141. Ibid., p. 33.

142. Ibid., pp. 65-67.

143. See Michael Reisman, "The Danger of Abandoning Taiwan," *New York Times,* August 28, 1976.

144. B. H. Ochlet, Jr., U.S. Ambassador to Pakistan, "How to Lose Allies," unpublished paper, May 19, 1970.

145. *Impact International* (London), September 12-25, 1975.

146. Mansfield, *China Enters the Post-Mao Era,* pp. 8-9.

147. Hugh Scott, *The United States and China: A Report by Senator Hugh Scott, Committee on Foreign Relations, United States Senate* (Washington, D.C.: U.S. Government Printing Office, 1976), pp. 2-3.

148. *New York Times,* June 8, 1976.

149. Ibid., August 4, 1976.

150. See then Vice-Chairman Hua Kua-feng's speech at the mass memorial meeting for Chairman Mao Tse-tung, *People's Daily* (Peking), September 19, 1976.

151. Ibid., December 26, 1976.

152. See press release no. 214 of the Mission to the United Nations of the People's Republic of China, New York, November 29, 1976.

153. Ibid., September 10, 1976.

154. See China's foreign minister's speech at the 1976 UN General Assembly.

155. George Modelski, *A Theory of Foreign Policy* (New York: Published for the Center of International Studies, Princeton University by Praeger Publishers, 1962), p. 9.

156. See Chou En-lai's speech, *New York Times,* July 18, 1972.

157. See *New China News Analysis,* domestic service January 12, 1973, translated in the Foreign Broadcasting Information Service (FBIS) on January 15, 1973.

158. *Washington Post,* December 19, 1976.

159. *New York Times,* November 3, 1976.

160. *New York Times,* November 11, 1976.

161. *Peking Review,* April 8, 1977.

162. *New York Times,* March 18, 1977.

163. *Washington Post,* February 28, 1977.

164. *New York Times,* April 11, 1977.

165. *New York Times,* April 12, 1977.

166. *Washington Post,* February 27, 1977.

167. *Washington Post,* December 22, 1976.

168. Ibid.
169. Ibid., April 29, 1977.
170. Ibid.
171. *New York Times*, May 13, 1977.
172. Ibid.